SPORTS AND HOBBIES
DOT MARKERS
ACTIVITY BOOK

30 illustrations of Sports and Hobbies(Basketball, Football, Baseball, Hockey, Drones, Music, Drawing, Cars, Bike Riding, Gaming & Many more.) dot marker activity and coloring book pages

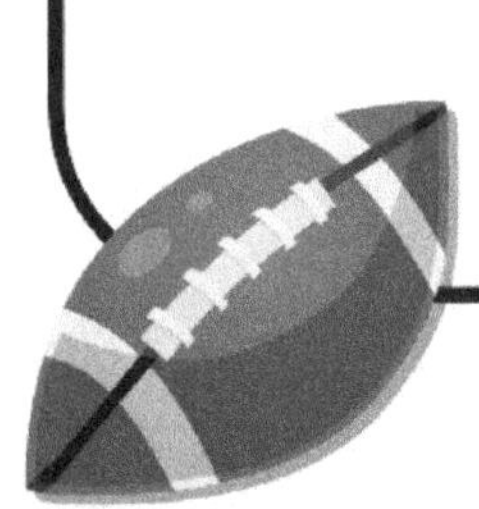

THIS BOOK BELONGS TO ___

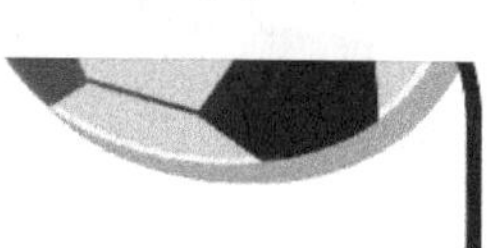

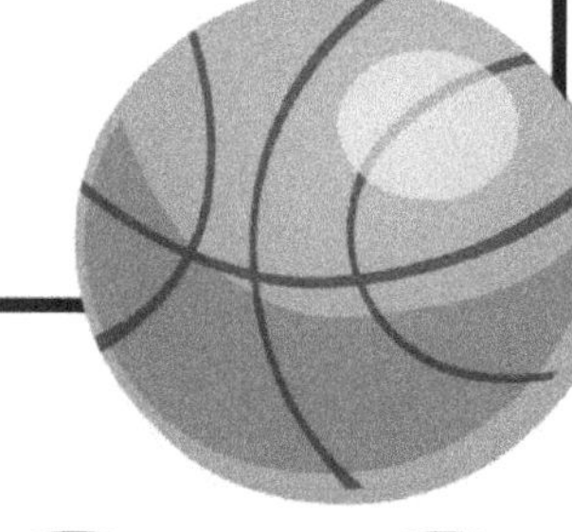

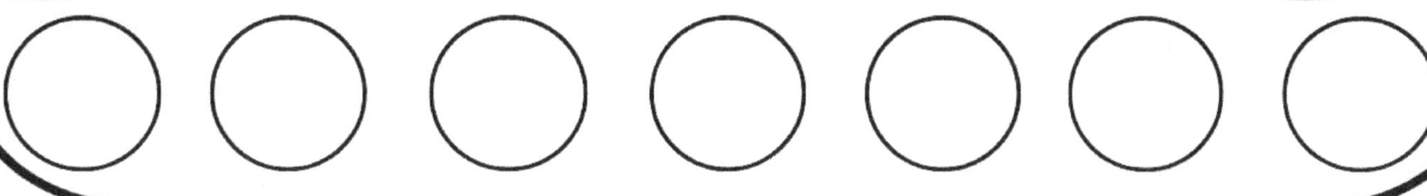

Test Your Color

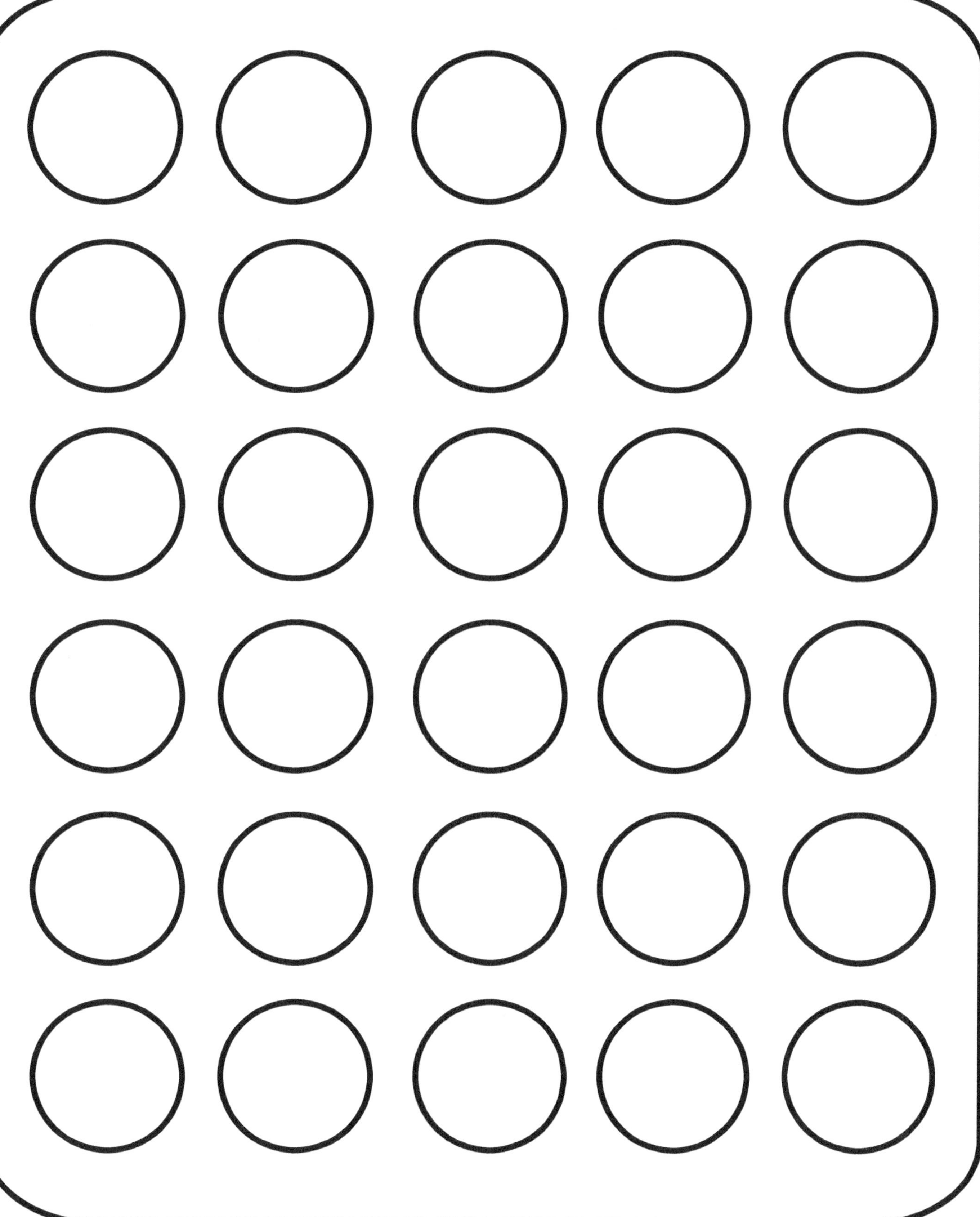

BASKETBALL

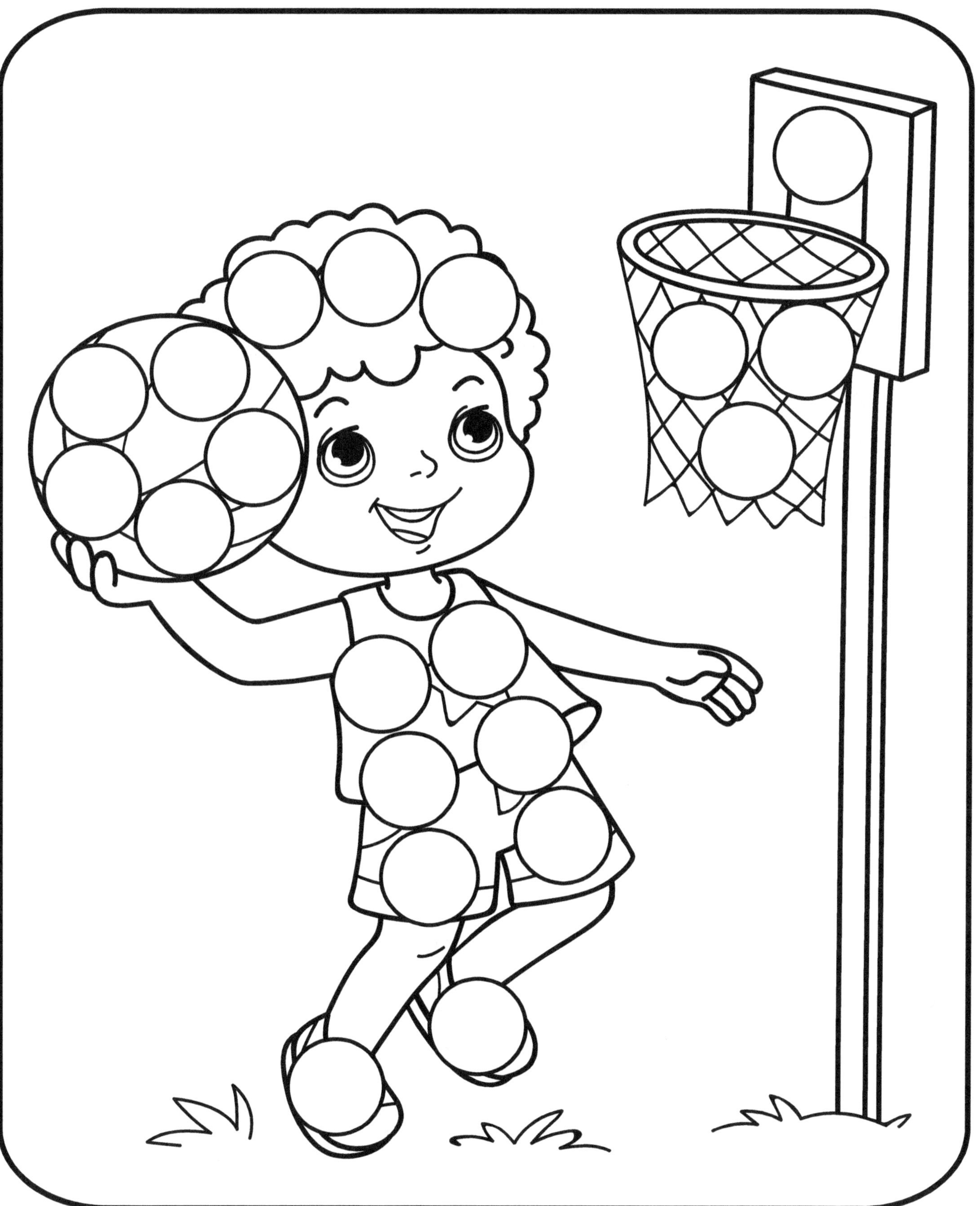

BASKETBALL

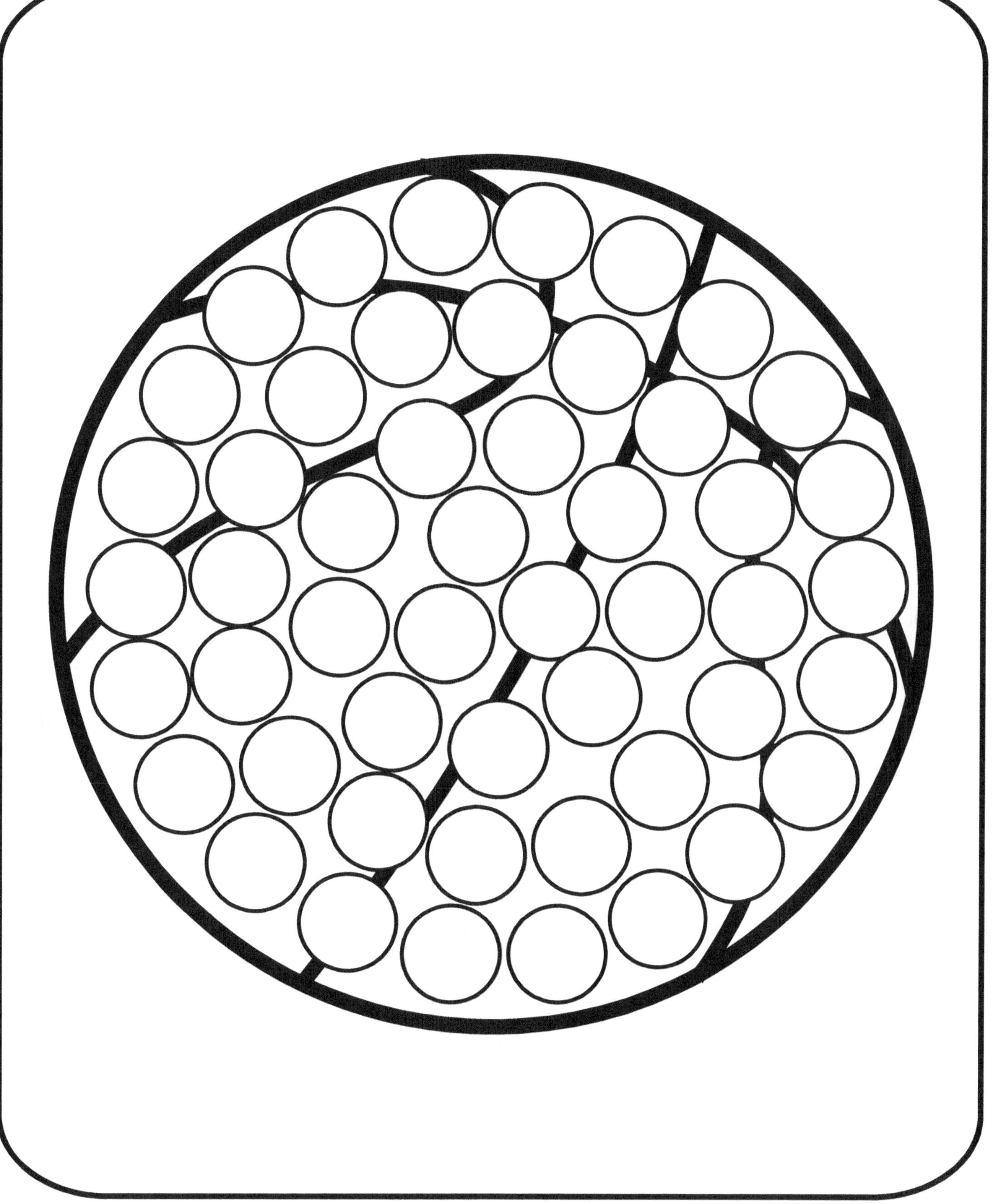

BASKETBALL

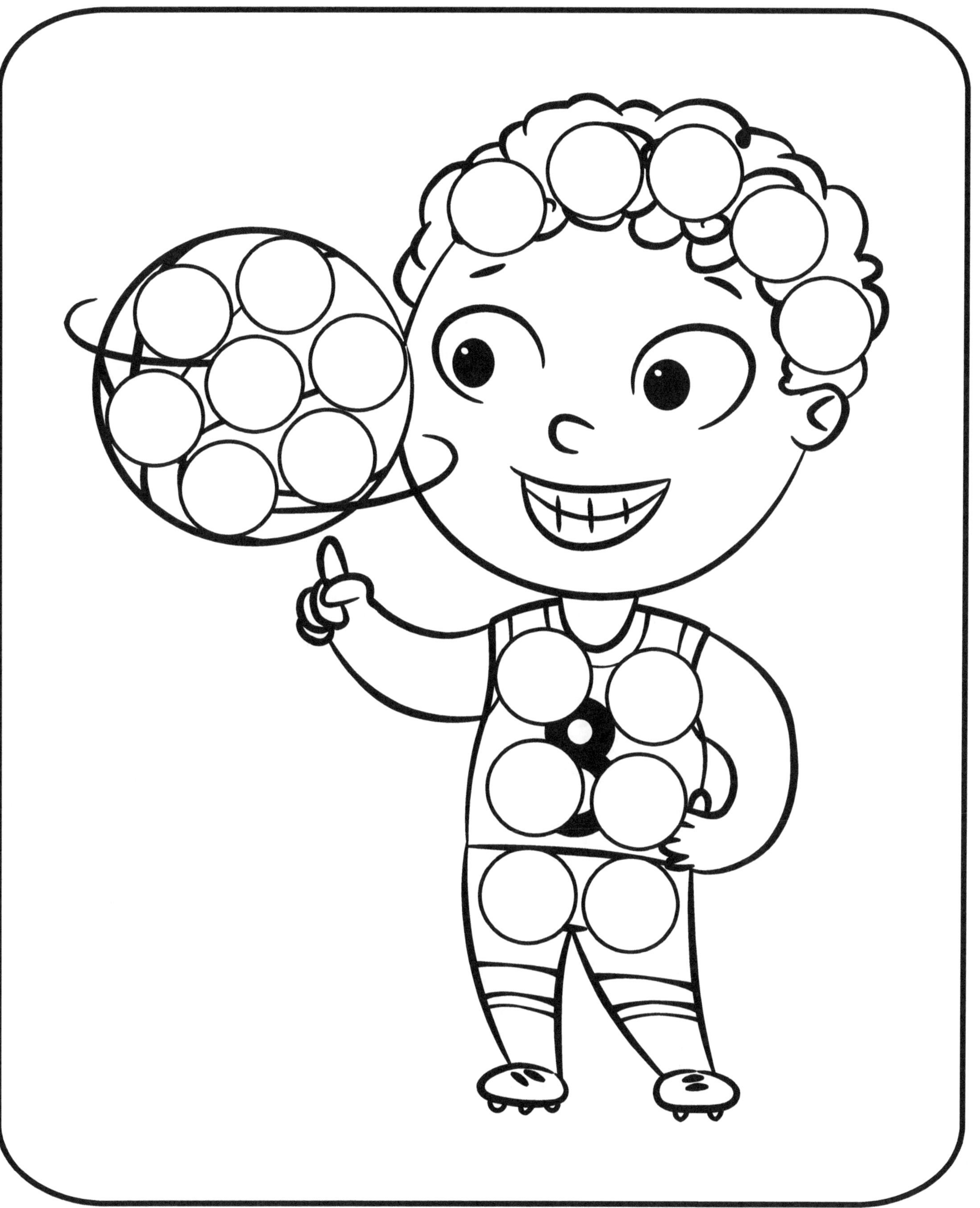

SOCCER

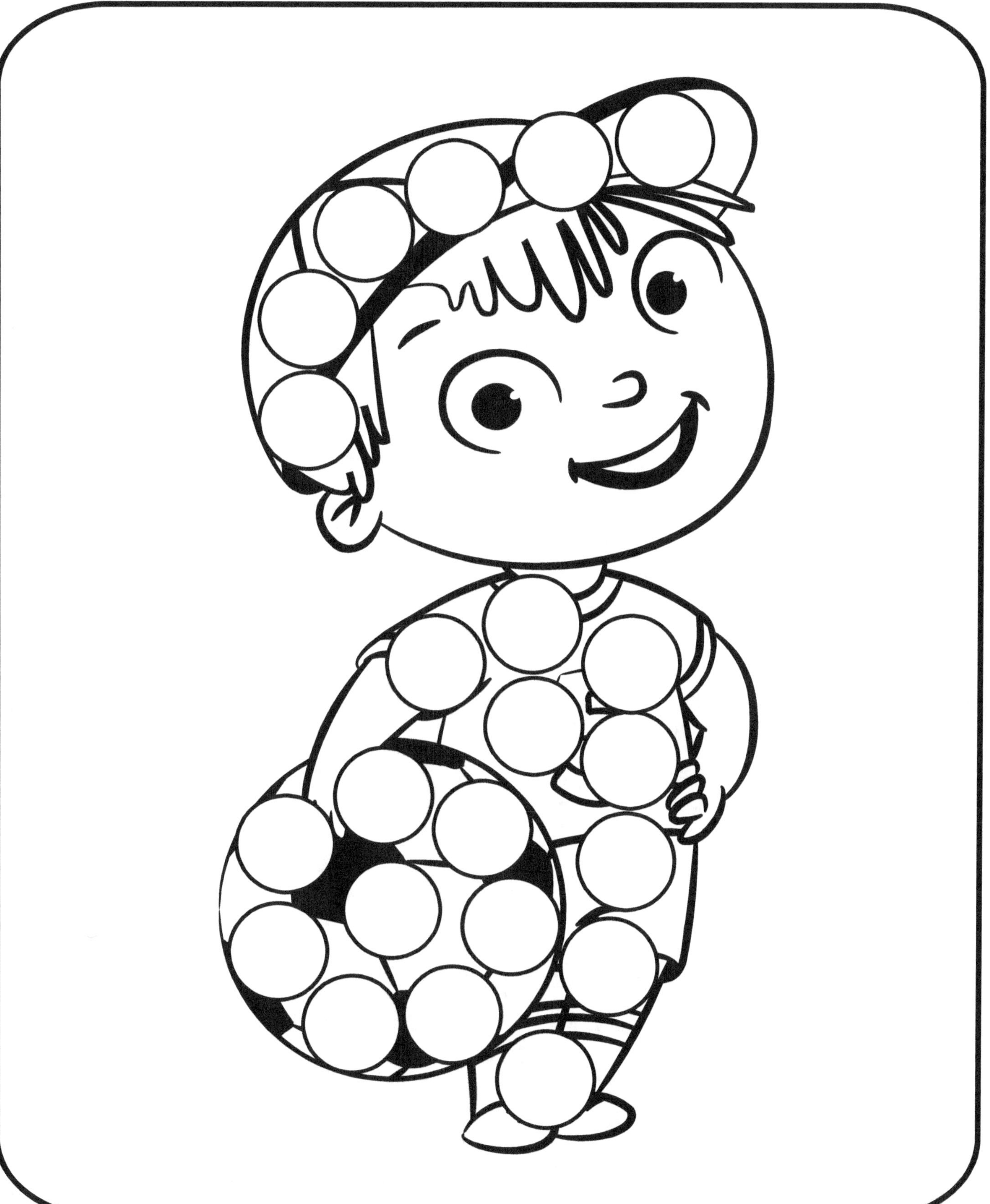

SOCCER

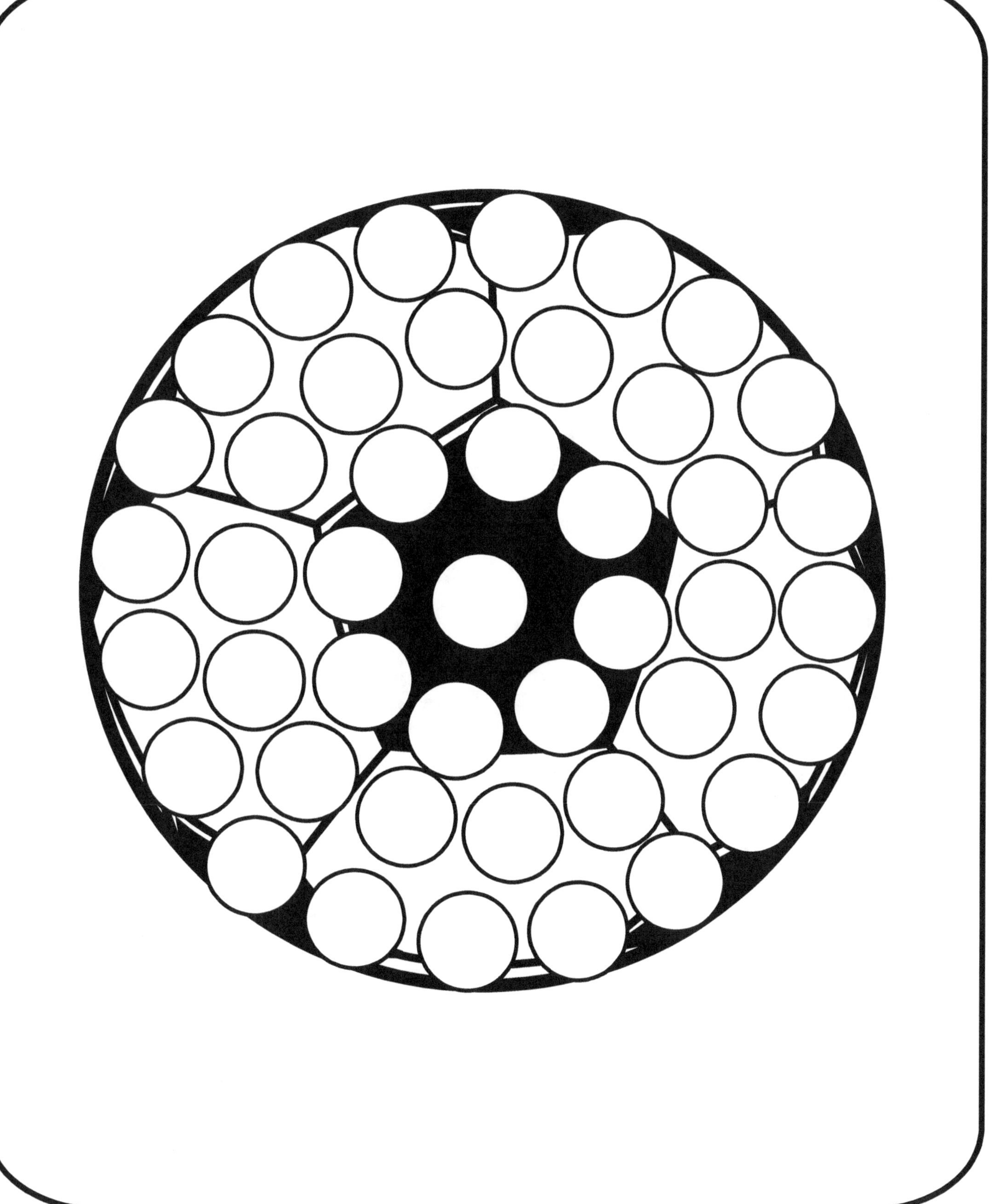

FOOTBALL

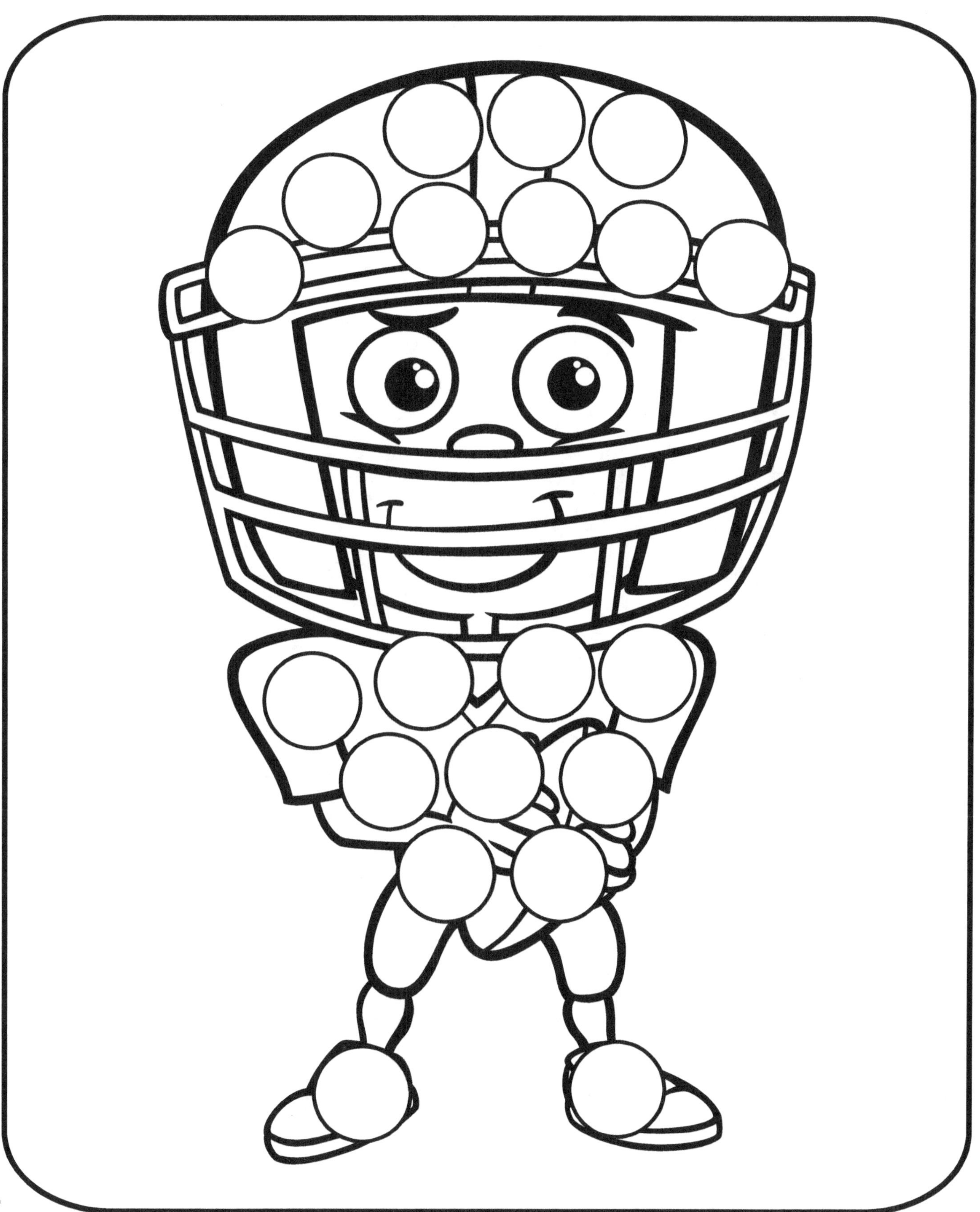

FOOTBALL

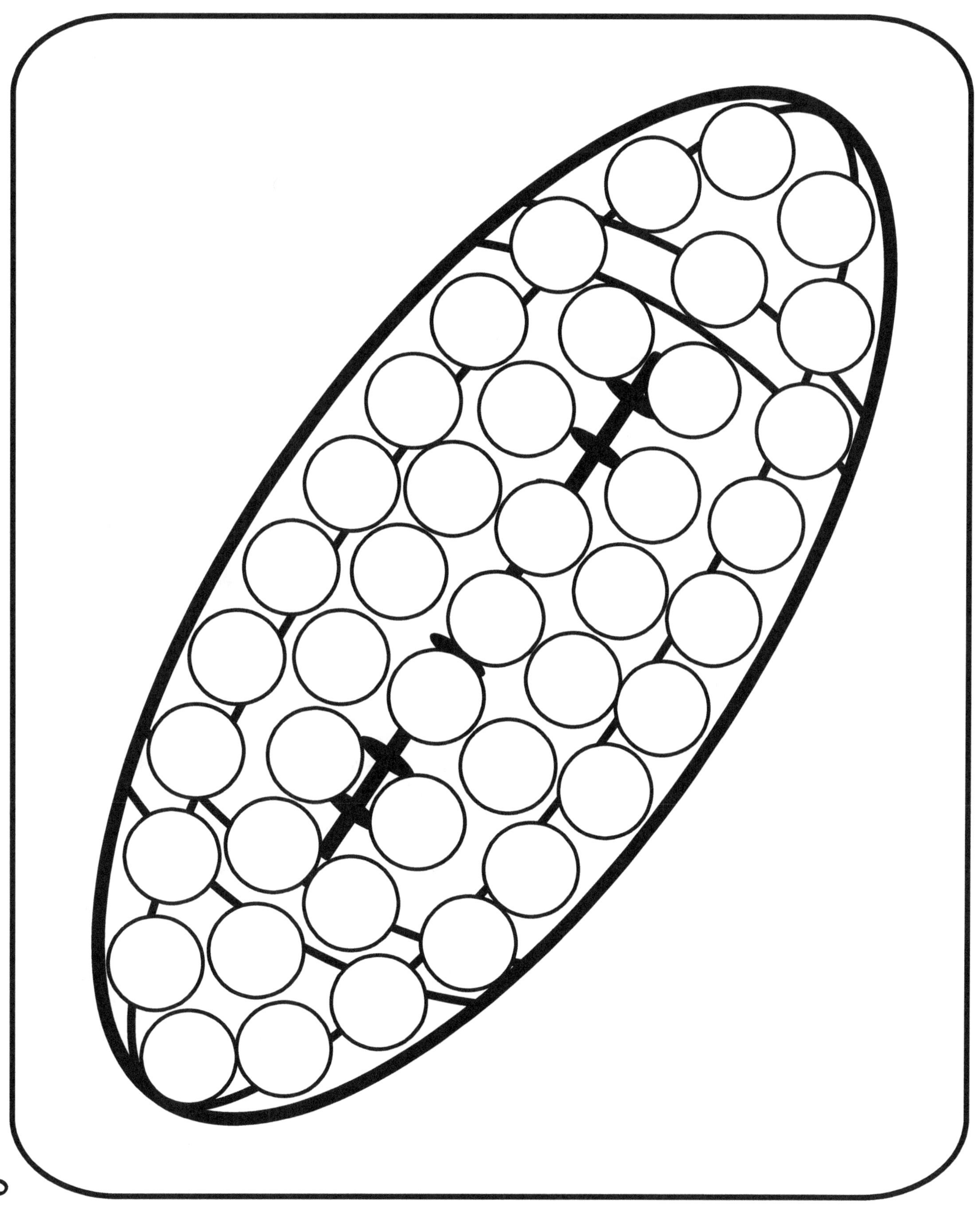

ICE HOCKEY

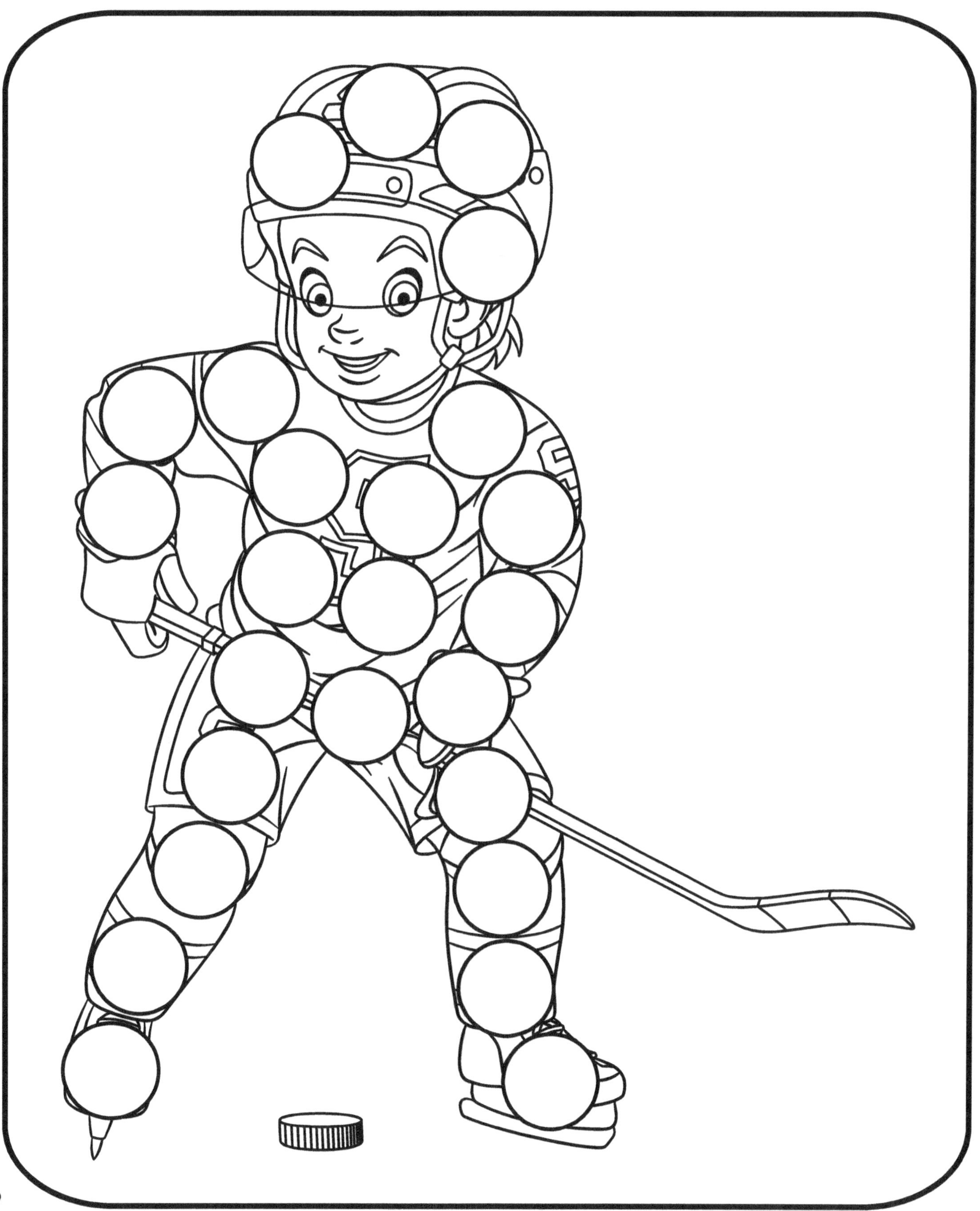

GOLF

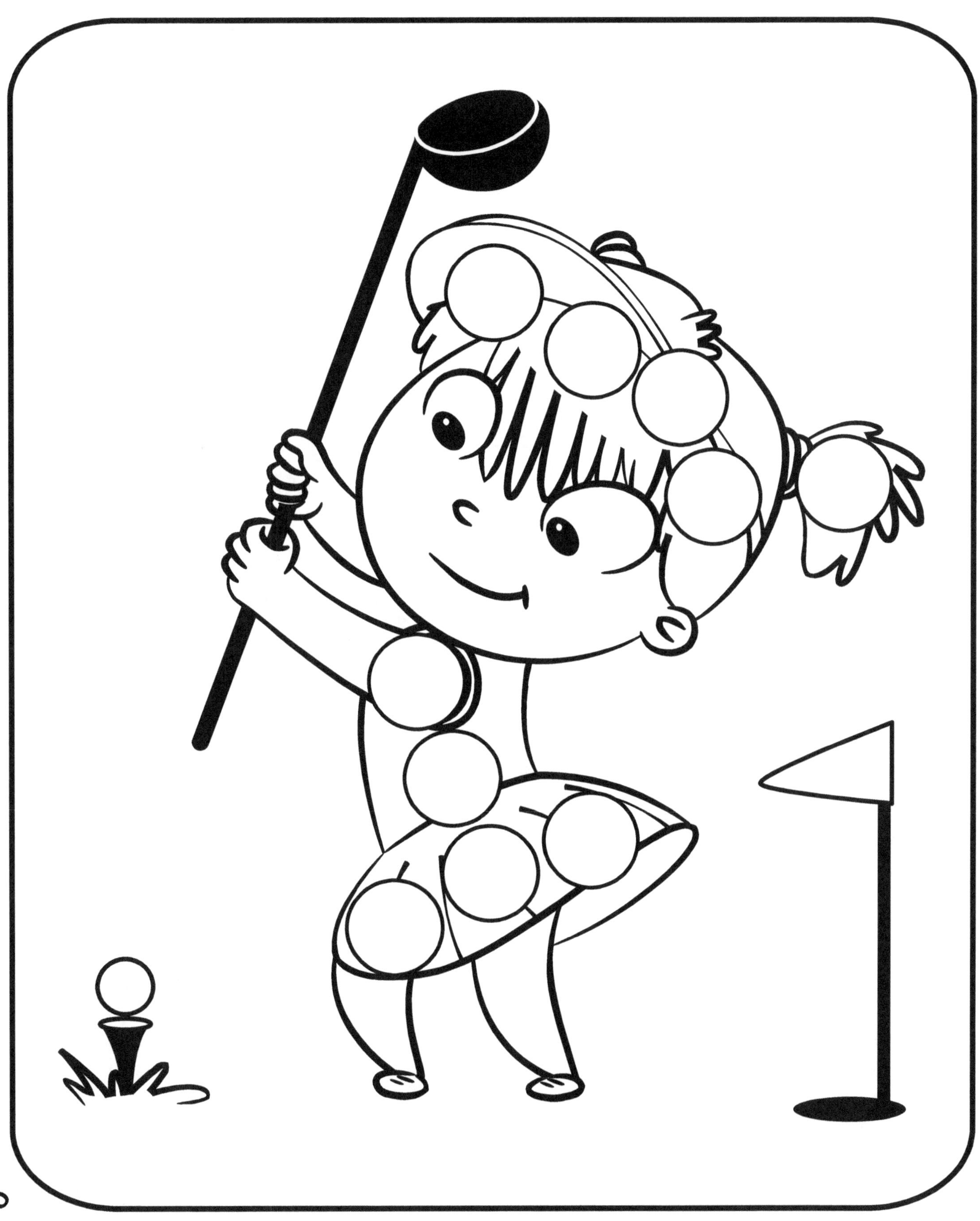

BASEBALL

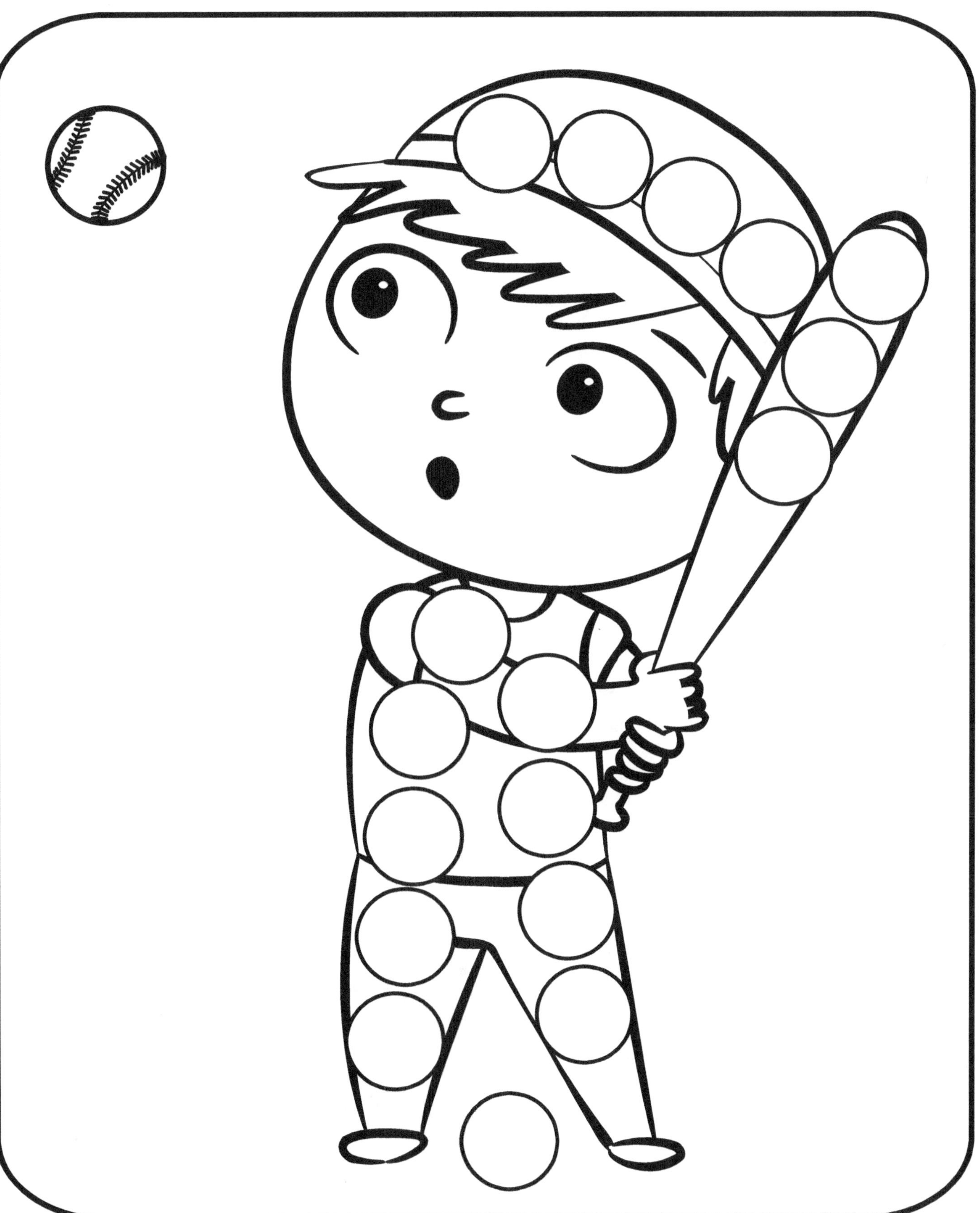

BASEBALL

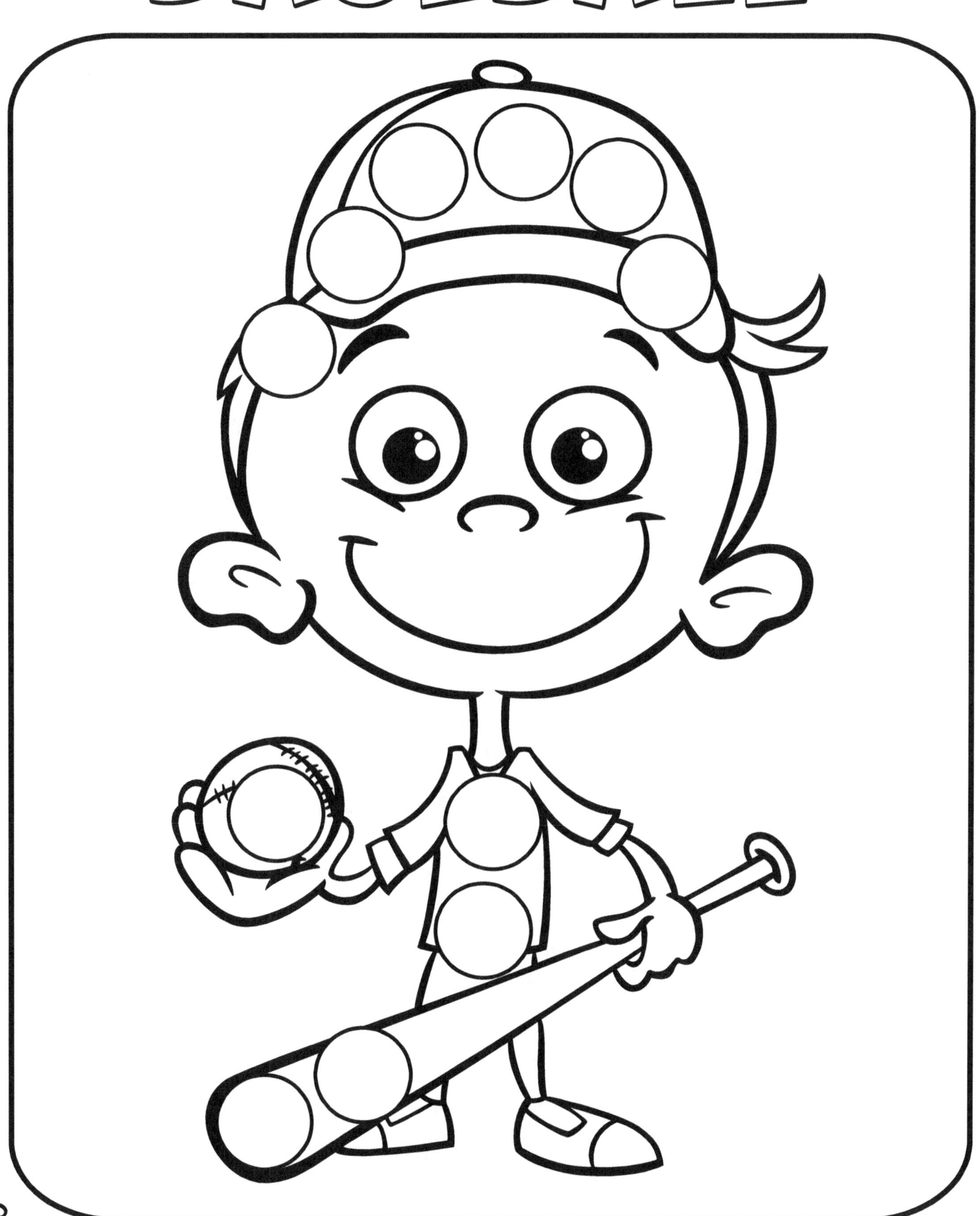

POWERLIFTING

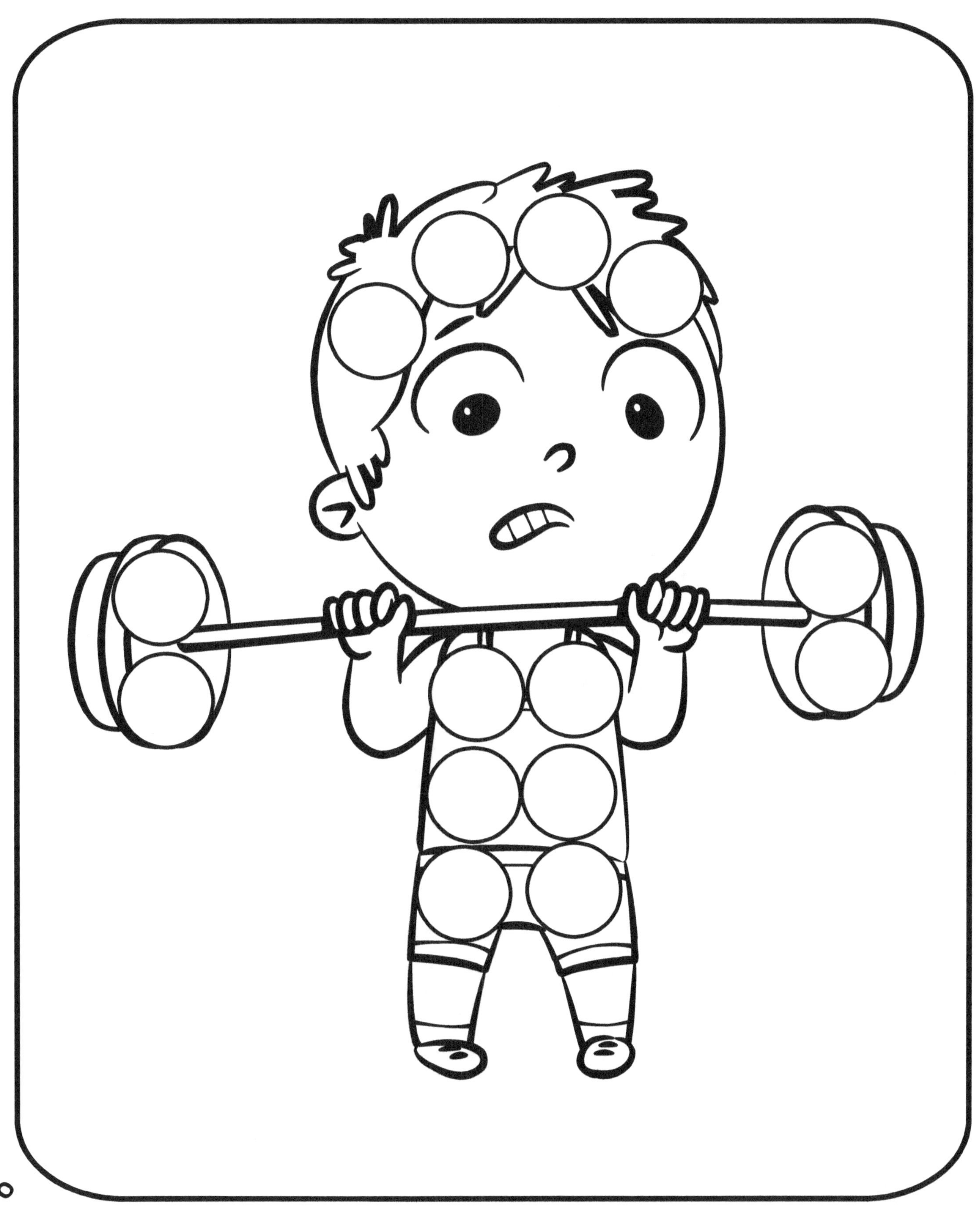

ICE SKATEBOARDING

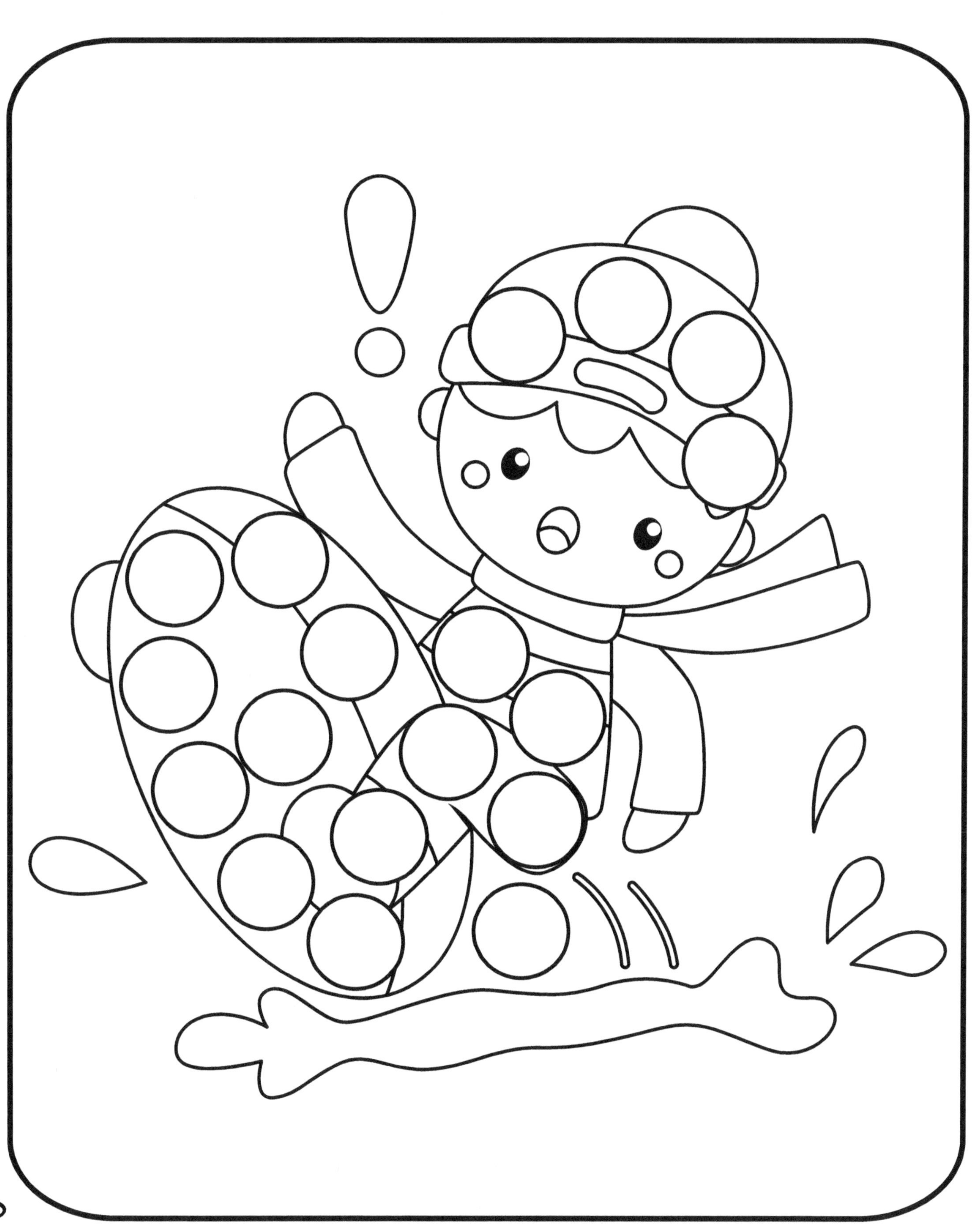

ICE SKATEBOARDING

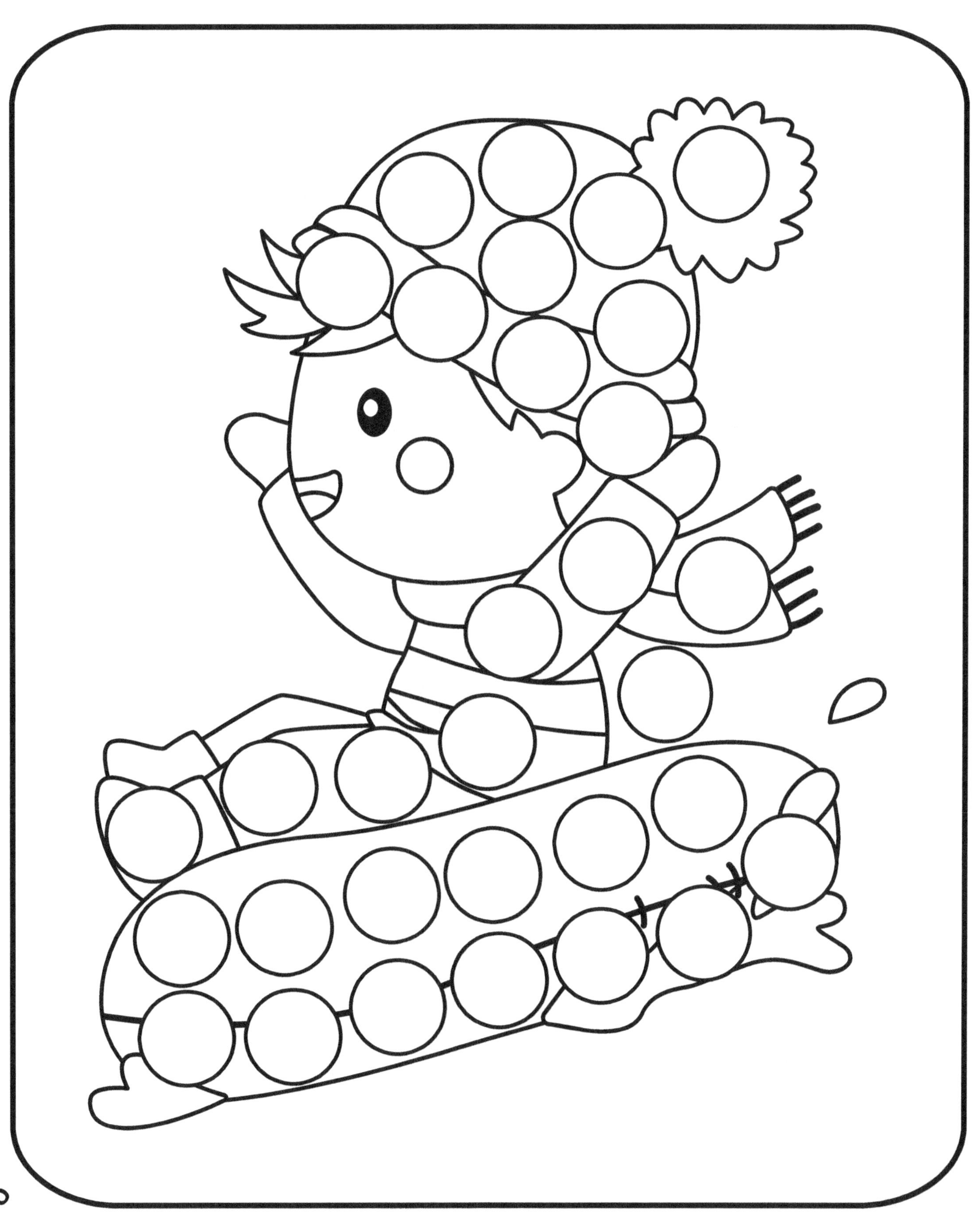

BADMINTON

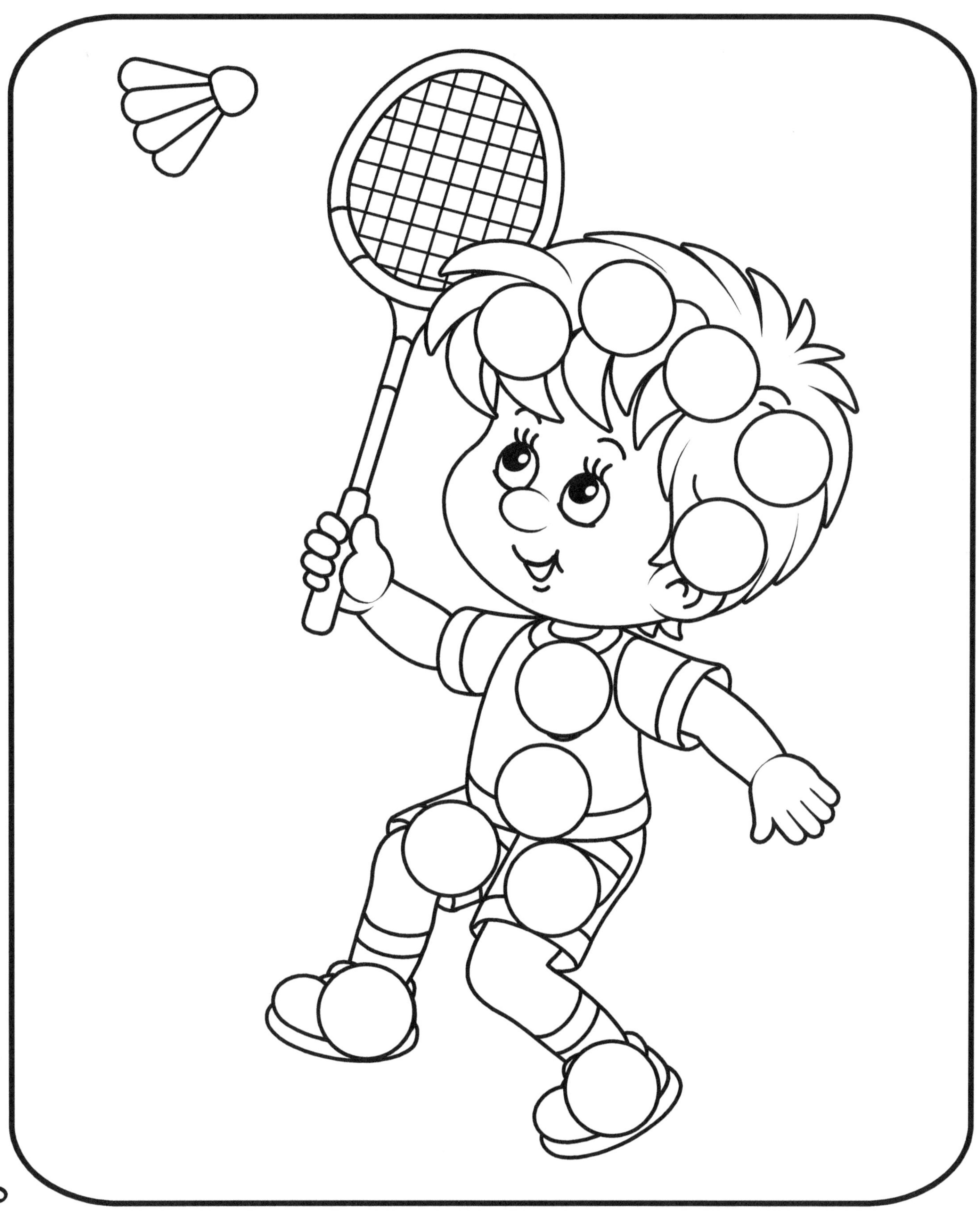

BADMINTON

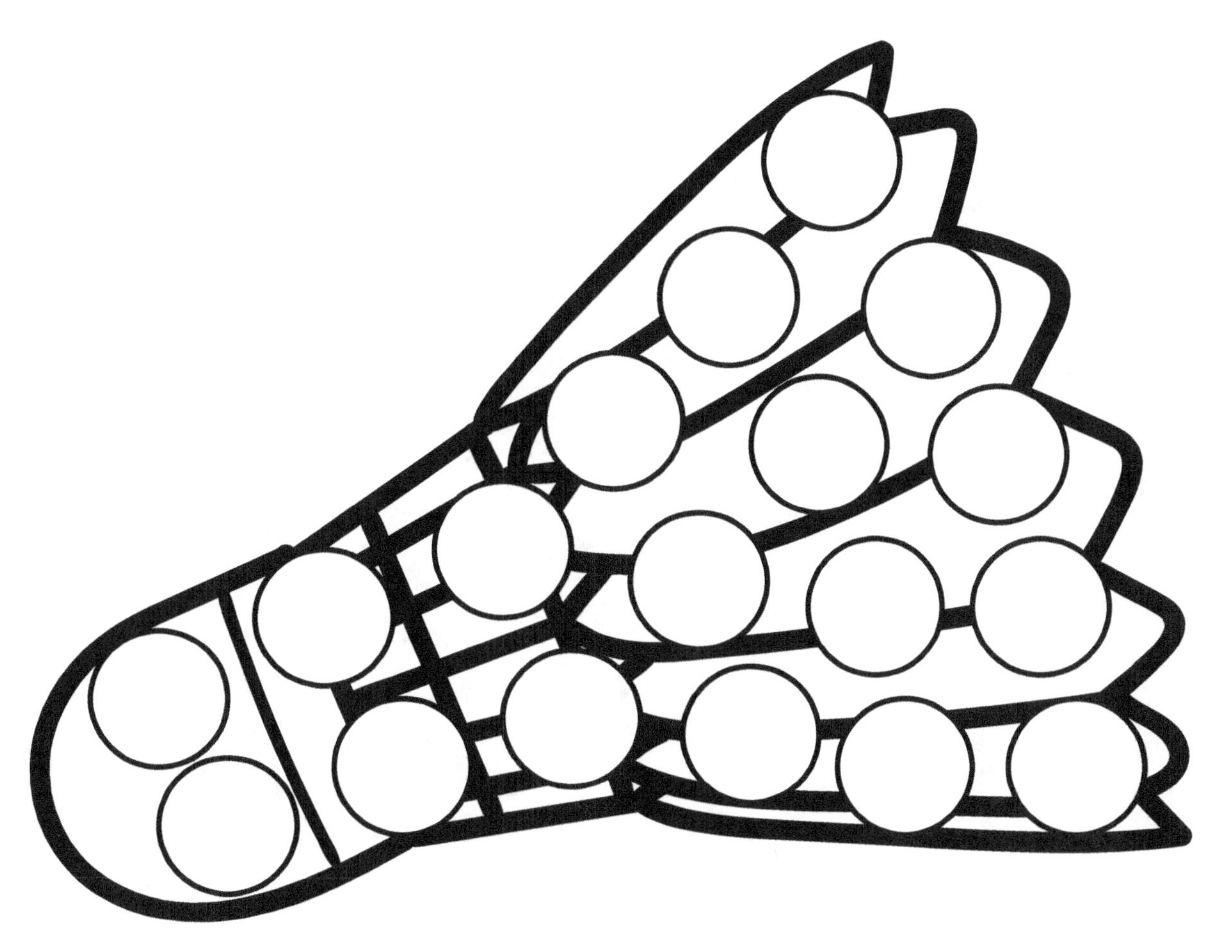

TENNIS

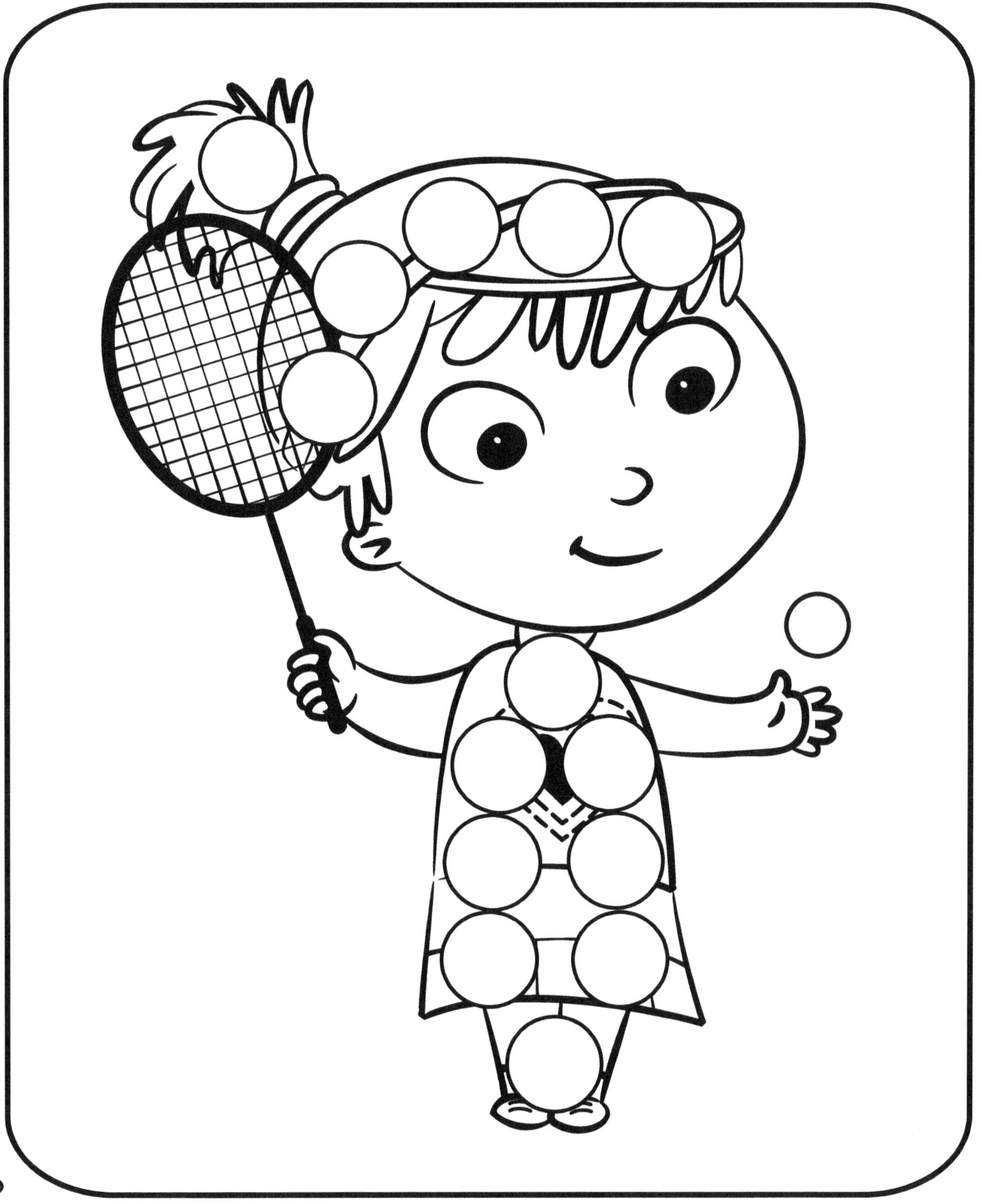

WINNING TROPHY

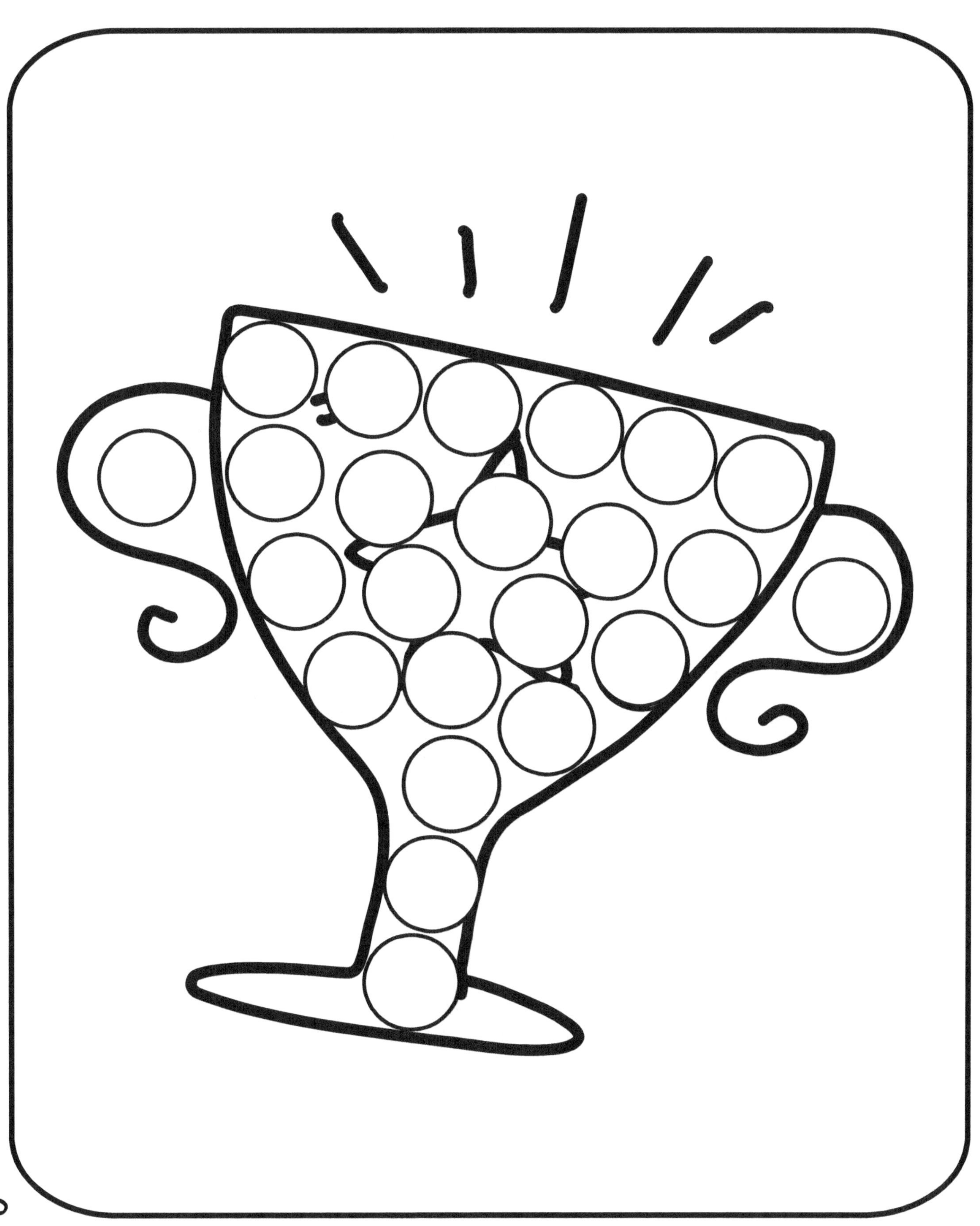

DRONE

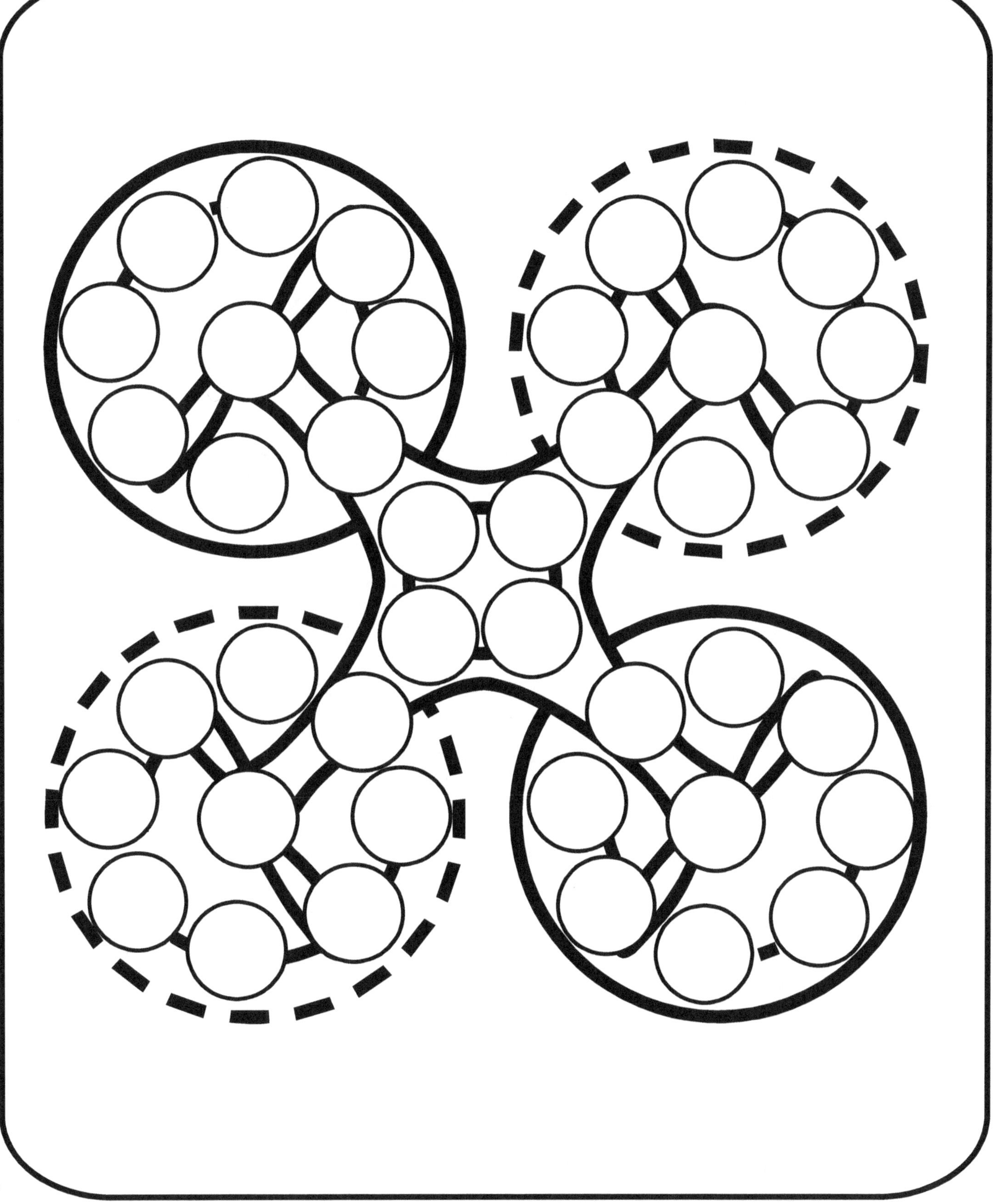

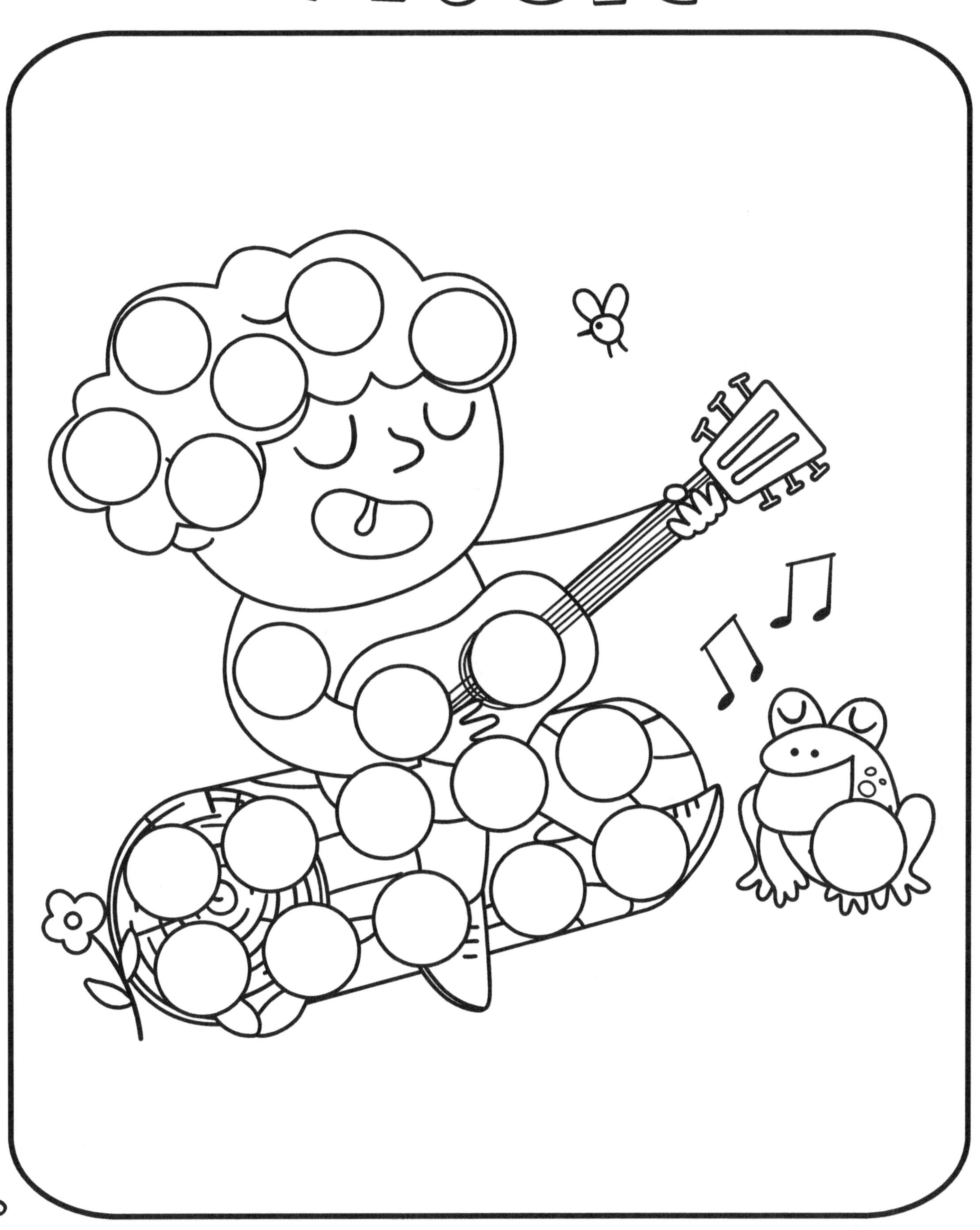

MUSIC

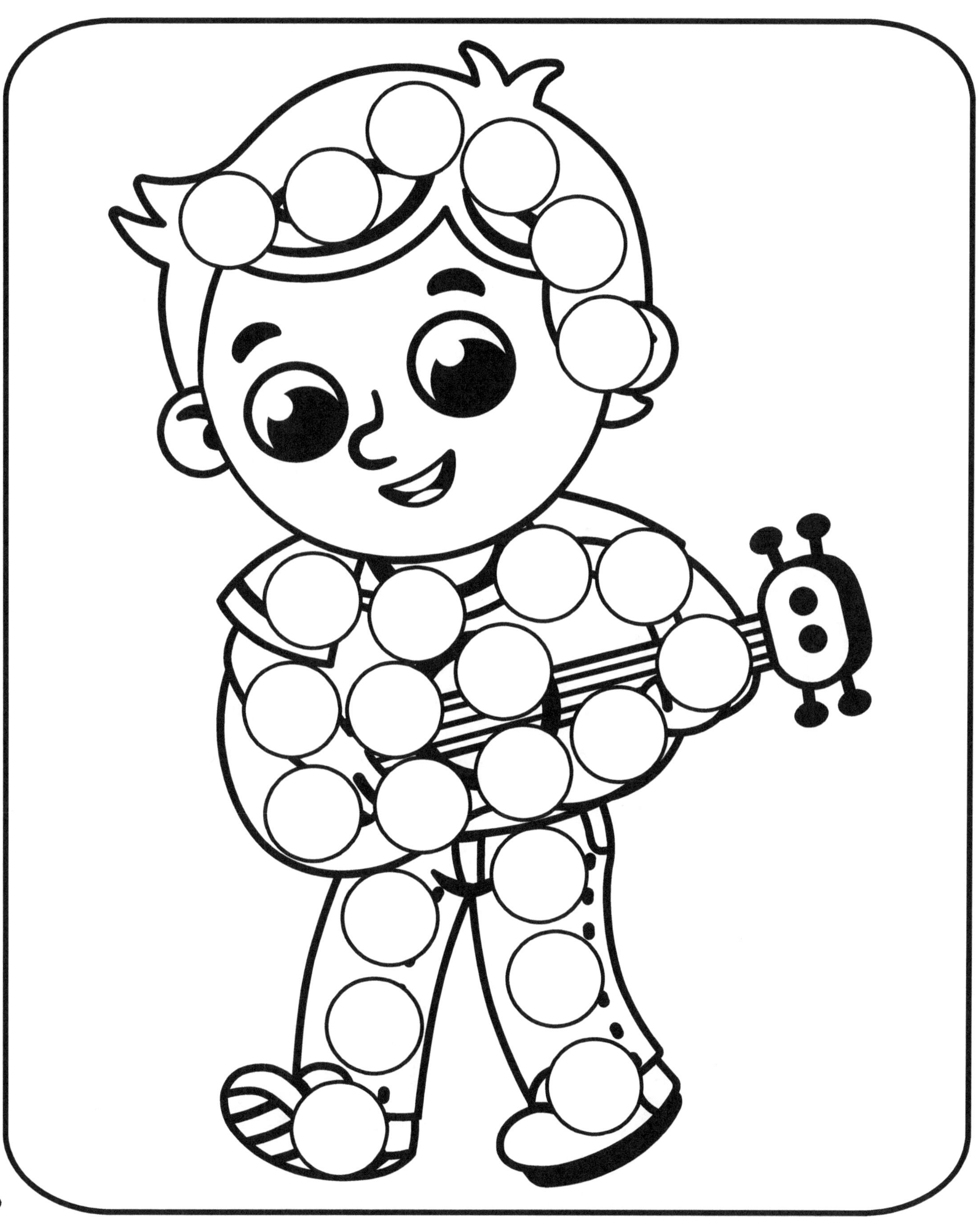

MUSIC

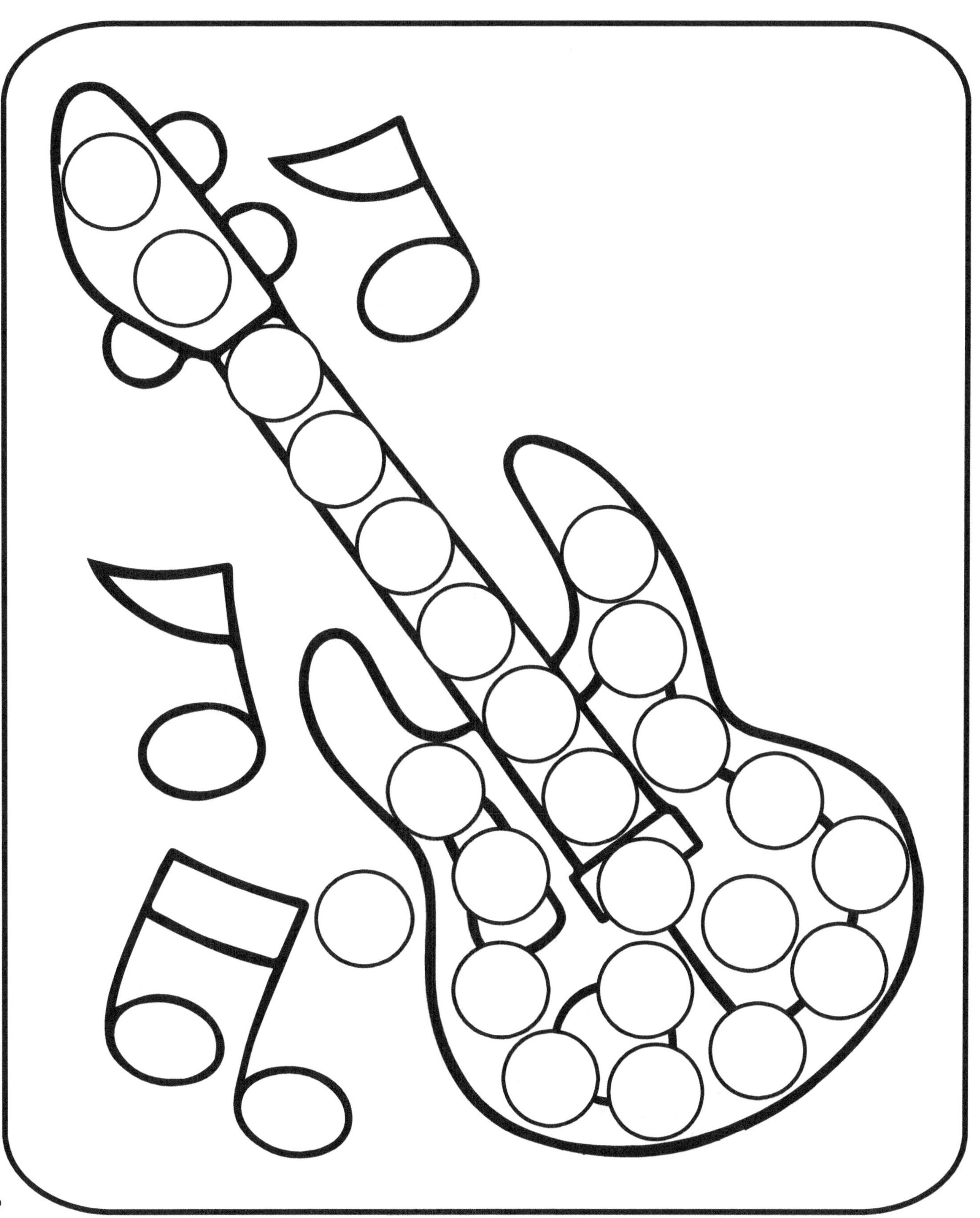

DRAWING

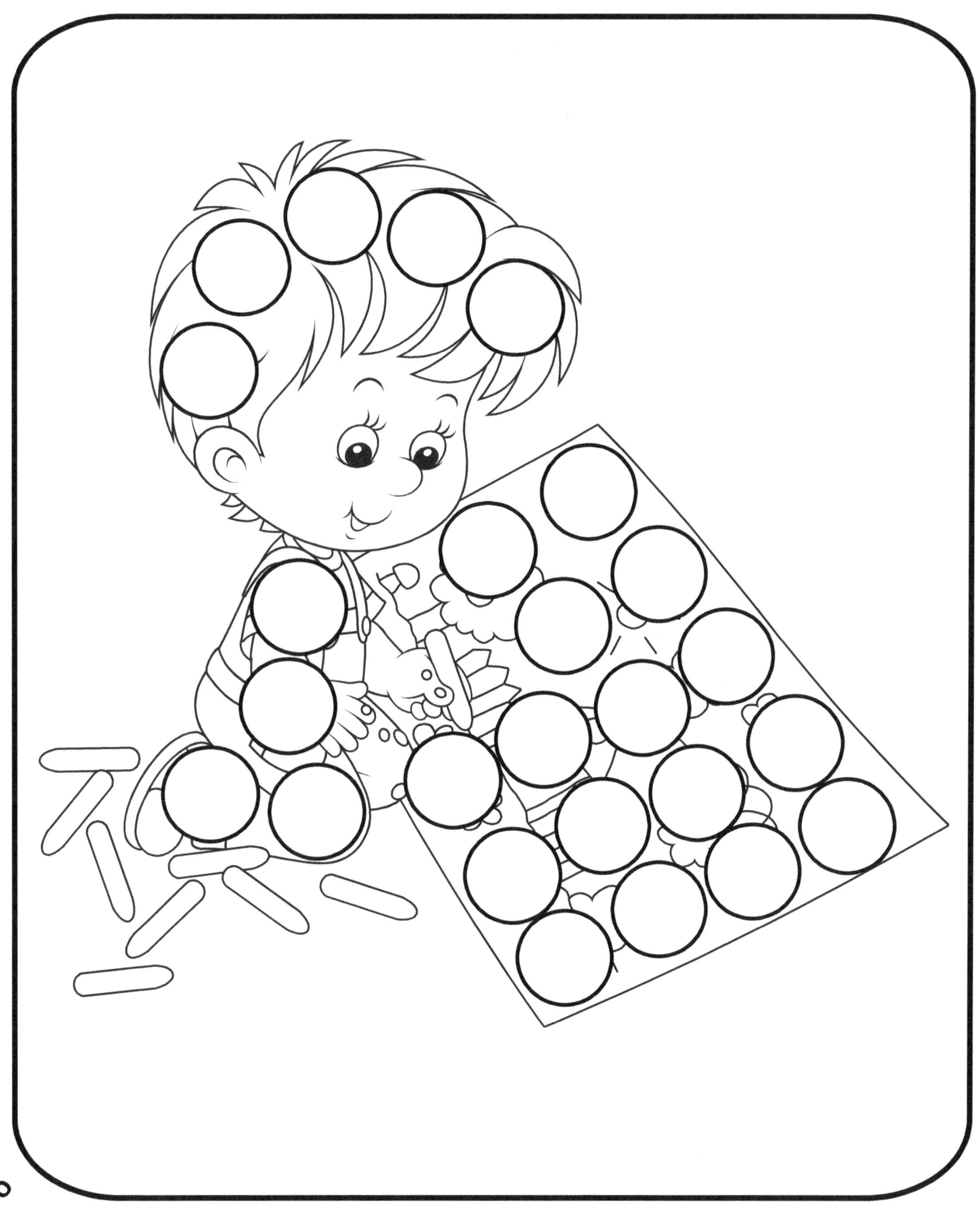

CAR

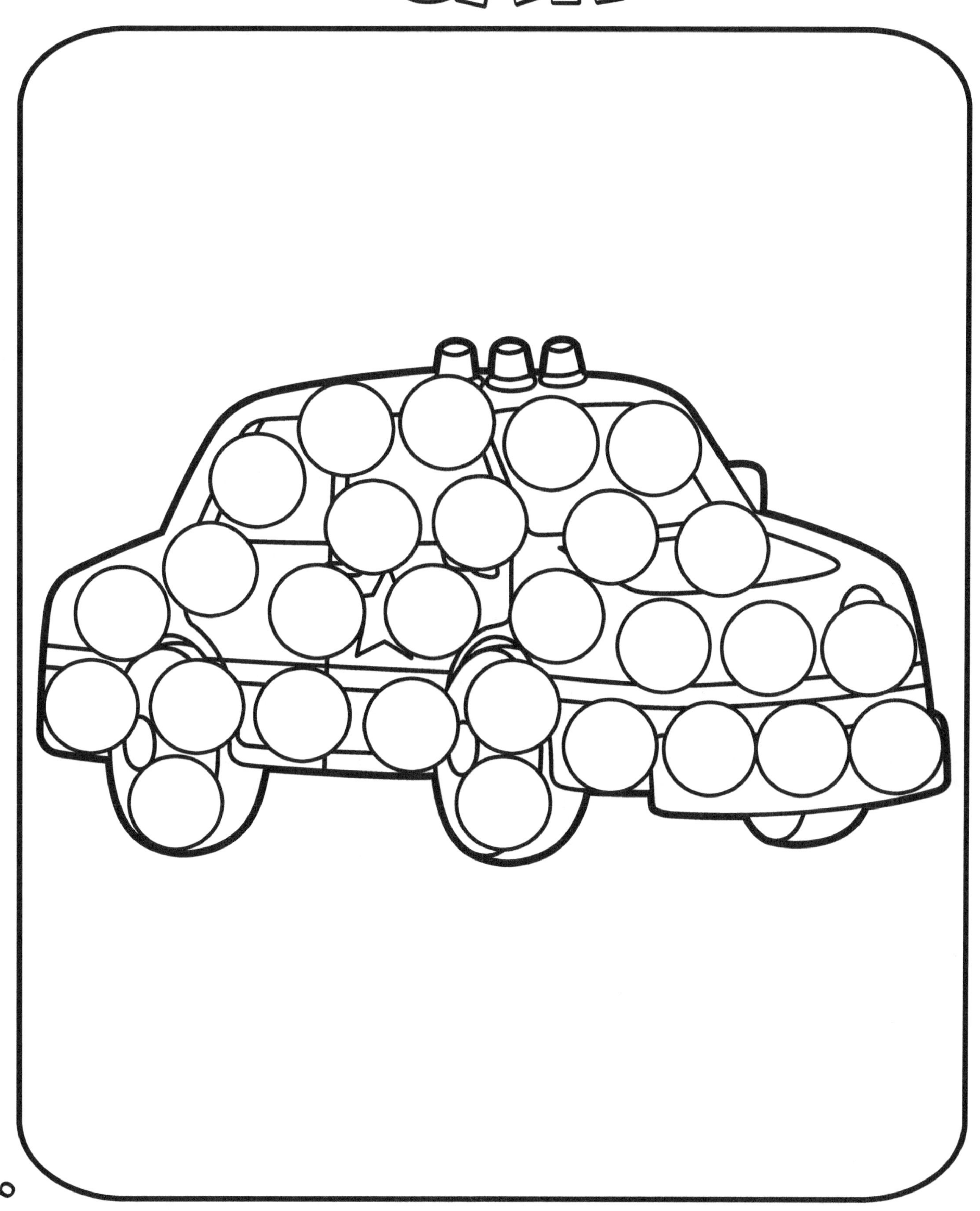

CAR

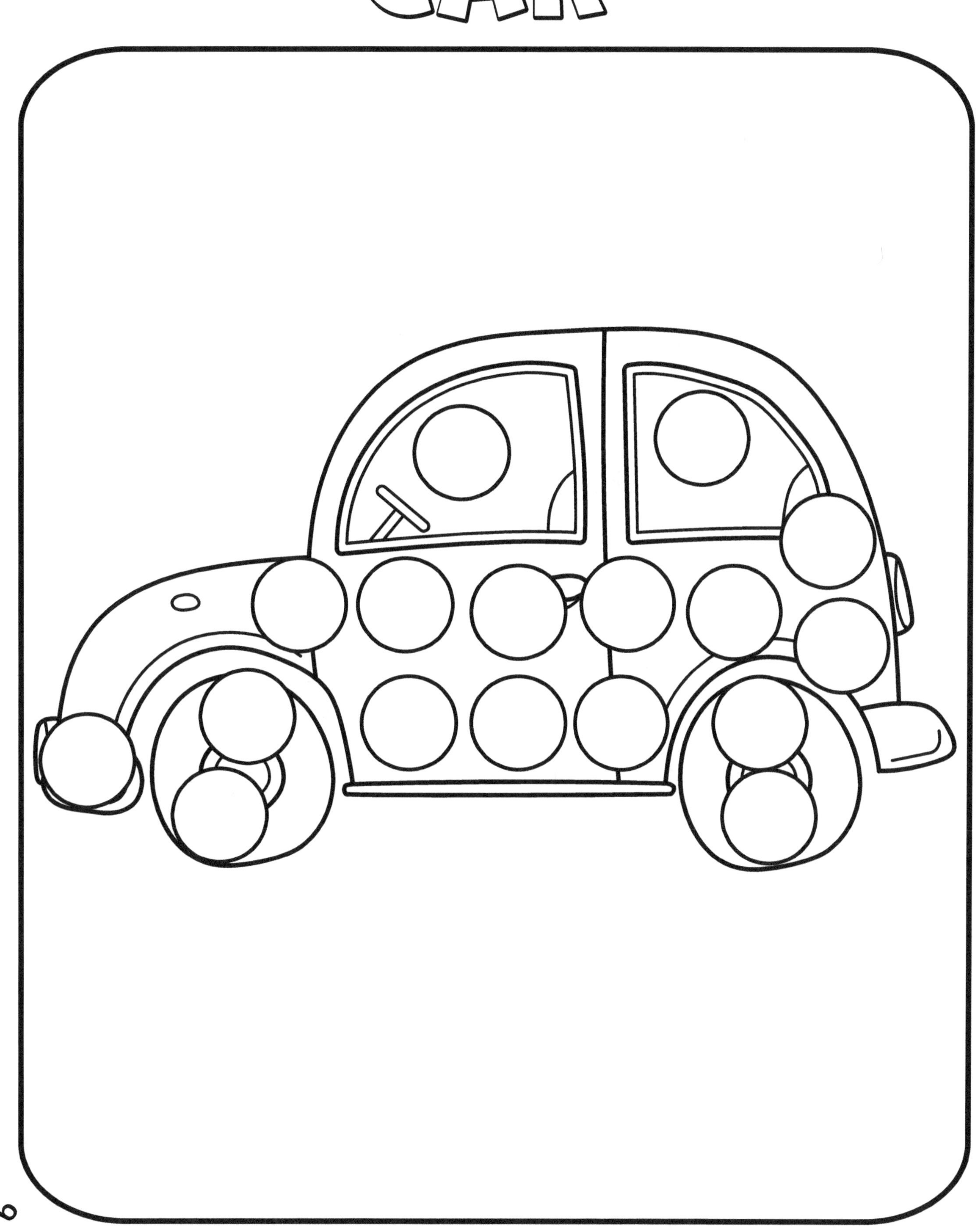

BYCYCLE RIDING

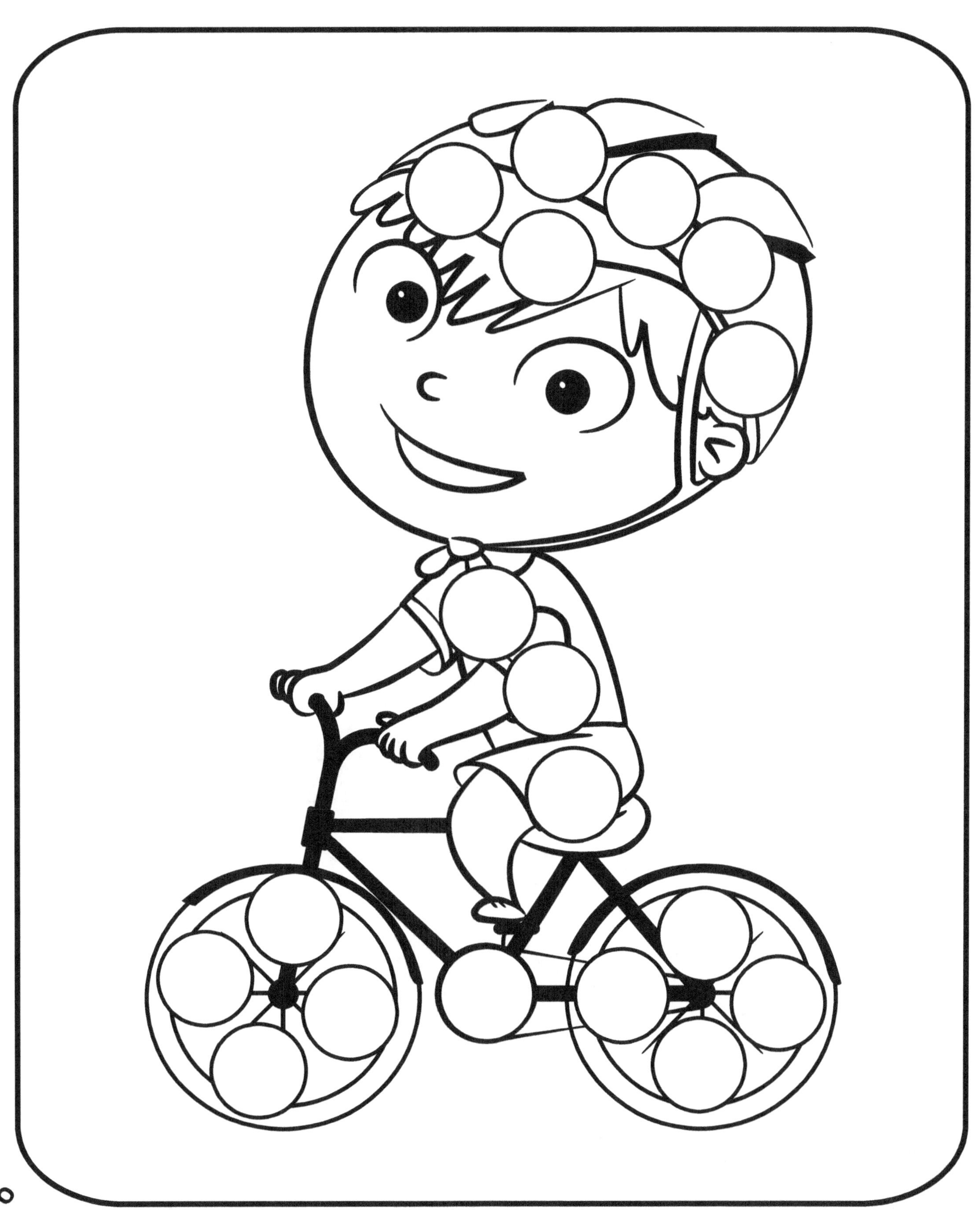

BYCYCLE RIDING

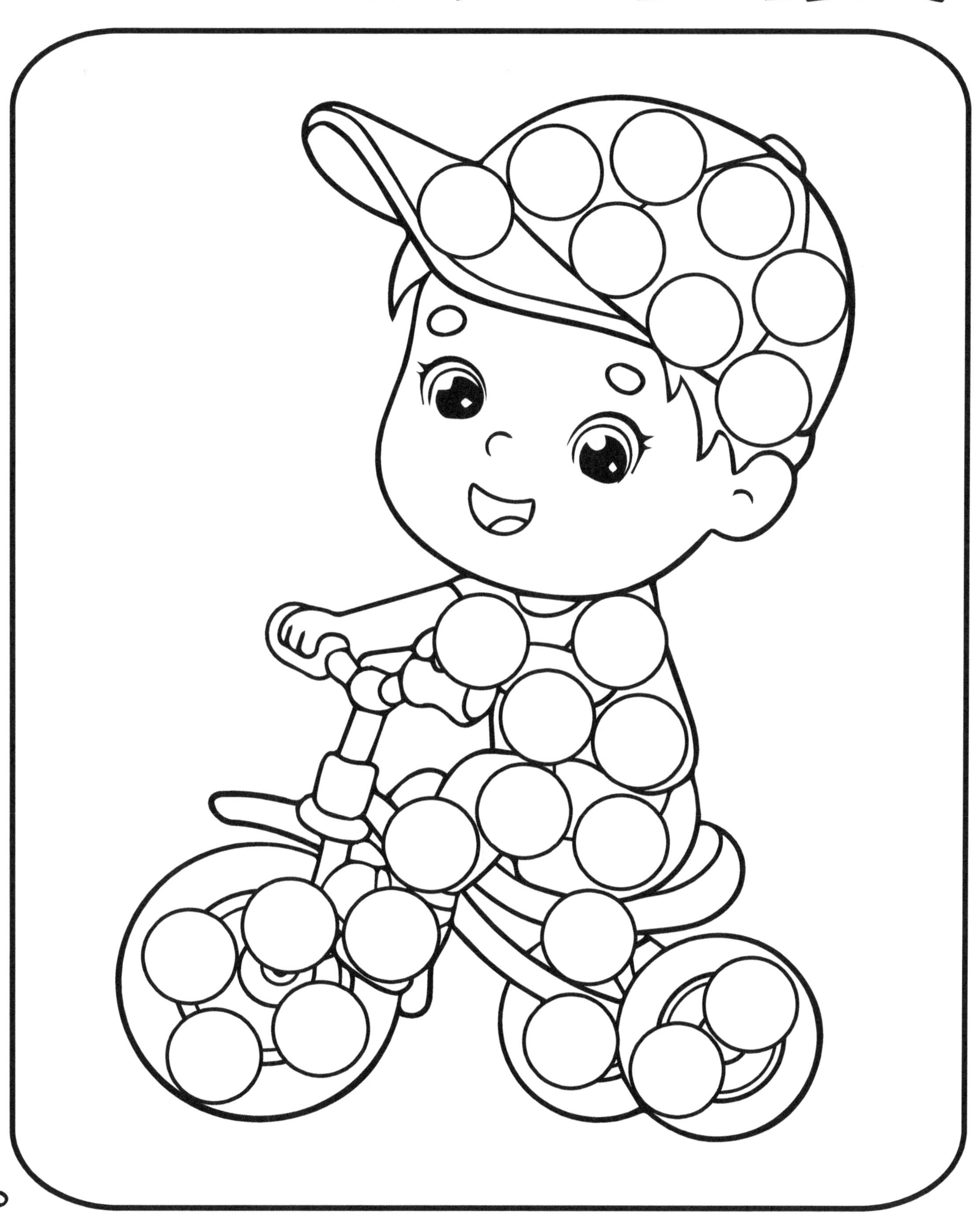

BIKE RIDING

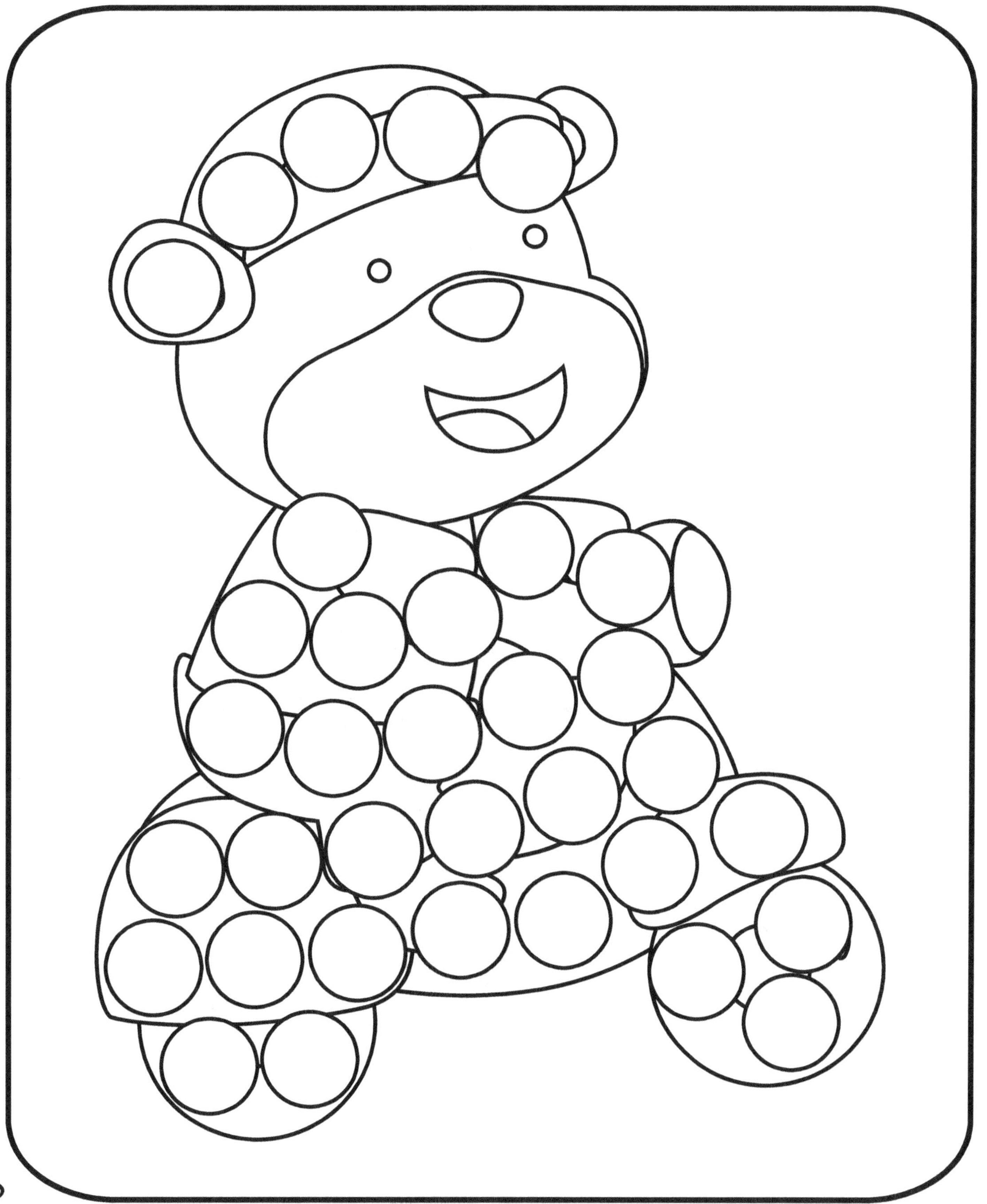

GAMING DEVICE

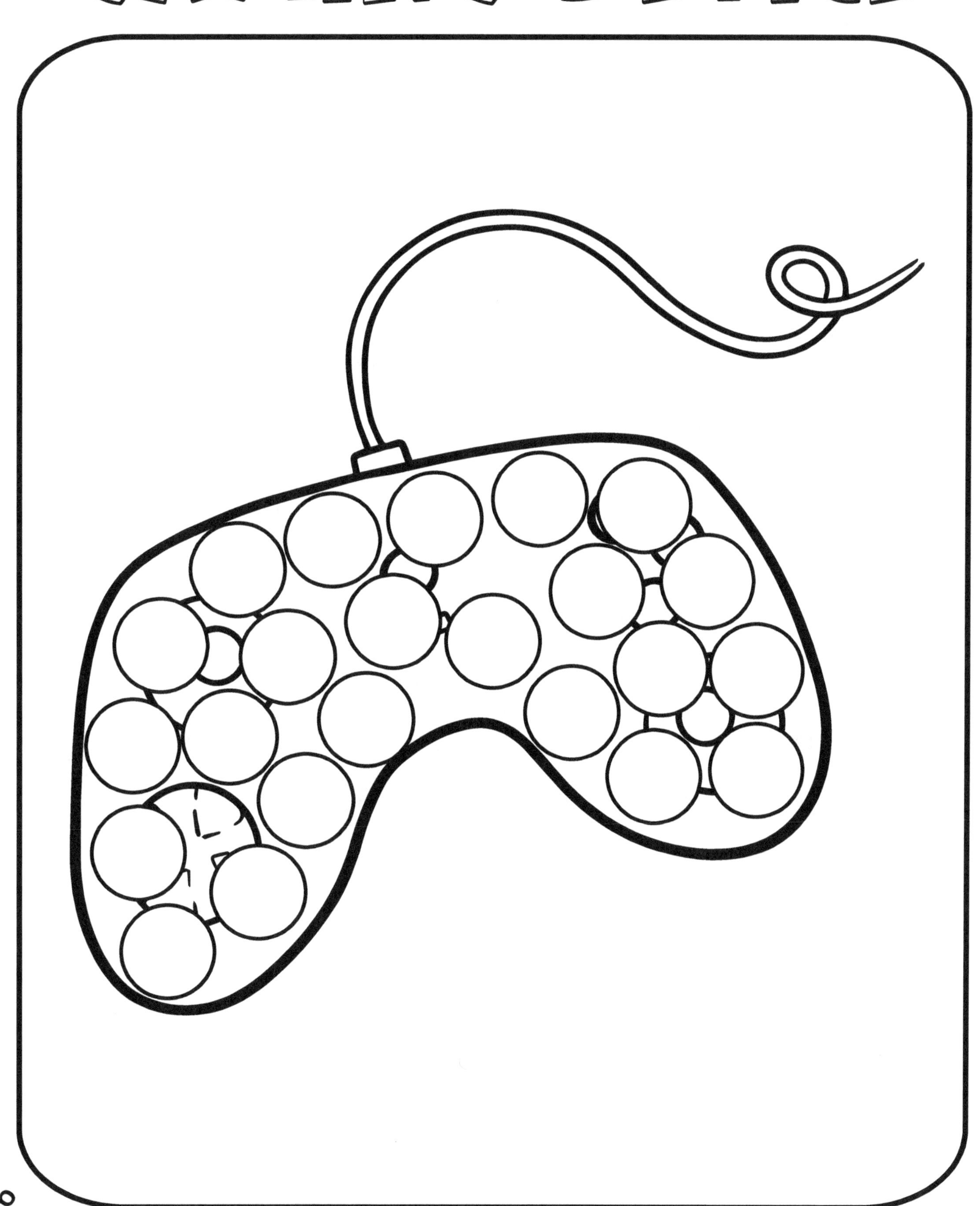

GAMER

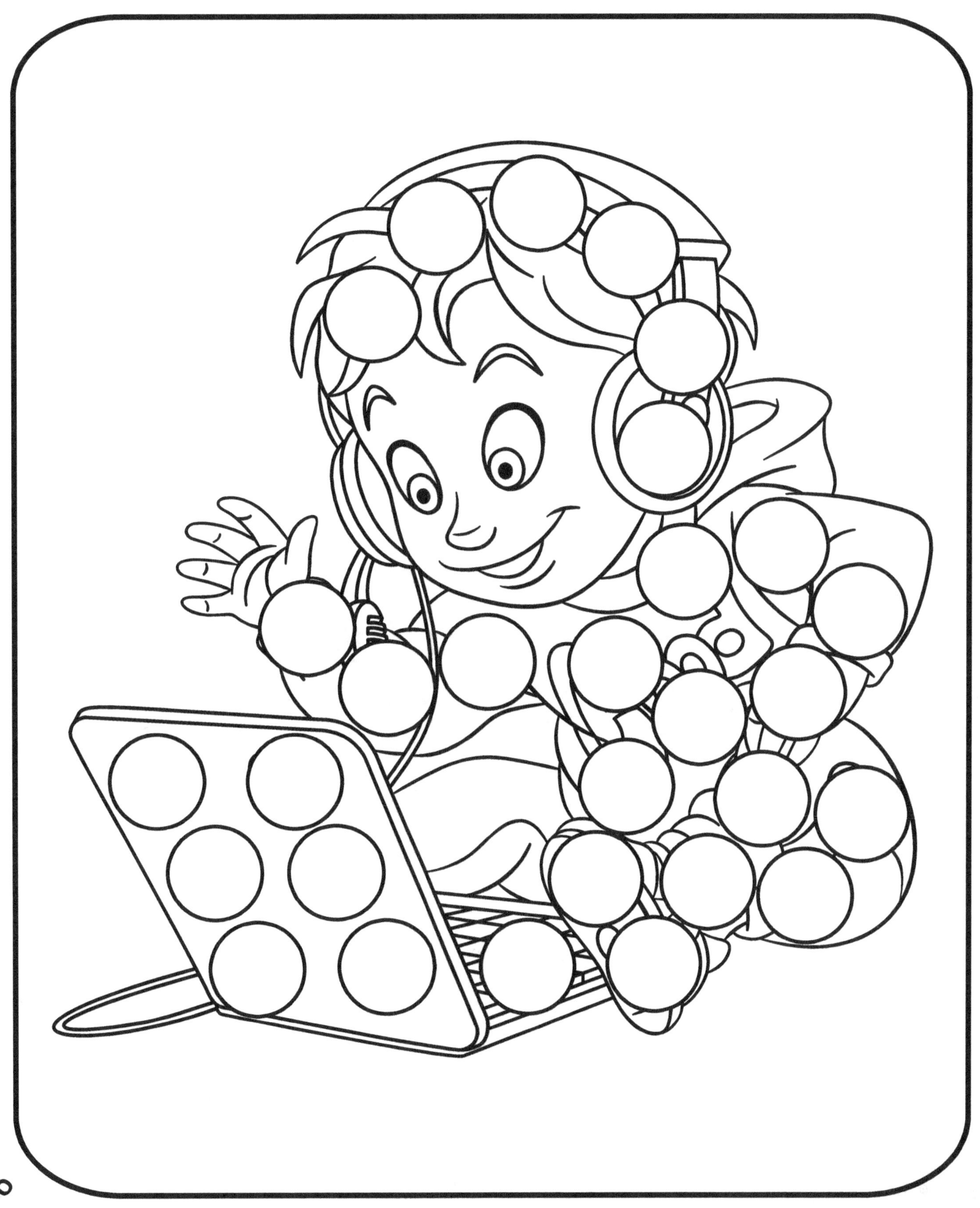